THE WONDER BOOK
OF
THINGS TO DO

[*Fox Photos.*

DIVING REFLECTIONS.

THE
WONDER BOOK
OF
THINGS TO DO

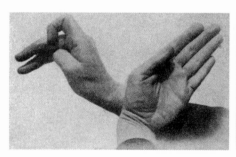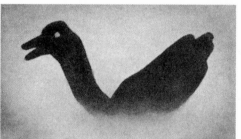

WITH EIGHT COLOUR PLATES AND
NEARLY 300 DIAGRAMS AND ILLUSTRATIONS

Third Edition

W A R D ,   L O C K   &   C O . ,   L I M I T E D
LONDON AND MELBOURNE

The information provided in this book is a general overview of the games, sports, activities and facets as recommended and published in 1936. The Publishers shall have no liability with respect to any harm, loss or damage, caused by, or alleged to be caused by, or in any way arising from, or alleged to be arising from information contained in this book. It is not an instruction manual and is presented as general information and should not be considered as a replacement for qualified and professional advice.

First published in Great Britain by Ward Lock & Co., Limited
This edition first published in Great Britain in 2008 by Cassell Illustrated,
a division of Octopus Publishing Group Ltd,
2–4 Heron Quays, London E14 4JP

Text, layout and design copyright © 2008 Octopus Publishing Group Limited
Octopus Publishing Group is a division of Hatchette Livre (UK)

Distributed in the U.S. and Canada by Octopus Books USA:
c/o Hachette Book Group USA
237 Park Avenue
New York NY 10017

All rights reserved. No part of this work may be reproduced or utilised in any form or by any means, electronic or mechanical, including photocopying, recording or by any information storage and retrieval system, without the prior written permission of the publisher.

A CIP catalogue record for this book is available from the British Library.

ISBN-13: 978-1-844-03656-1

Production: Caroline Alberti
Publisher: Mathew Clayton

Printed and bound in China

10 9 8 7 6 5 4 3 2 1

A POWERED FLYING MODEL.

COLOUR PLATES

A BALANCING FEAT.

CONTENTS

CONTENTS

[Fox Photos.

REPAIRING AND REPAINTING THE MODEL RAILWAY.

CONTENTS

[*Fox Photos.*

EXERCISES FOR FITNESS.

A TOBOGGAN RUN.

[*Mirrorpic.*

KEEPING THE FLAG AFLOAT.

[*Fox Photos.*

9

CONTENTS

FLYING MODELS.

To make flying models, construction must be lightened throughout. Components are built up from balsa strip and sheet, tissue covered.

[J. J. Ward.

THE CROCUS: CLOSED AND OPEN.

WONDERS OF PLANT LIFE

SOME PRACTICAL EXPERIMENTS

PLANTS do many strange things which would be very difficult for us to understand, could we not show by experiment what they are really doing.

The plant's mechanism works so silently and slowly that we sometimes almost forget that the plant is a living organism. We can understand an animal, because it breathes, eats, is active, and uses senses which show that it is very much alive. But while the plant really does most of these things, yet it does not appear to be doing any of them—unless we regard its quiet movement of growth as activity.

How Light Affects Plants

Sometimes, though, we see plants perform active movements, which may be slow, or more or less rapid. Some window plants will be seen to bend over towards the light. If we turn the other side to the light, the plant will then gradually upright itself and, if left for a while, it will eventually bend that side towards the window. The plant is really adjusting its structure to take the best advantage of the light available.

Light is essential to the plant, for, without it, it cannot form starch and sugar in its leaves, with which to make new growth. There are many ways in which plants utilize light. Crocus and tulip flowers will expand and close their blooms several times on a typical March or April morning. They will readily open to the bright sunlight, but will commence to close almost immediately when the clouds come up, or even when it becomes cold.

How to Make a Crocus Close its Flowers

If, on a sunny day in March, you cover a crocus plant in full bloom with a large flower-pot which has been cooled by dipping into cold water, in from fifteen to twenty minutes its flowers will all have closed. Then, if the sun is still shining, and you raise the cover, in from ten to fifteen minutes the flowers will have again all become fully expanded. This experiment really speeds up the more gentle action that an on-coming cloud would produce.

How to Make a Barberry Flower Hold a Pin

Some plant movements are instantaneous, like those of the leaves of the sensitive plant, or the stamens of barberry flowers — which when touched with a pin on a sunny day, will take it from your fingers and hold it.

[J. J. Ward.
A Barberry flower holding a large pin.

How to Show that Plants need Light to make Growth

We see, therefore, that both green plants and coloured flowers are much influenced by light. Indeed, they cannot grow for long without it. If you keep a plant in the dark, its leaves soon become a whitish-yellow colour, and those that develop later, get smaller in size. Soon it is obvious that the plant has become sickly. If, however, you bring it back into the light again, it will at once commence to revive, and its leaves will again become green.

In the same way, a potato when kept in a dark cellar will develop long, whitish shoots, bearing only fragments of leaves of the same pale colour. It may also form a few tiny potatoes about the size of peas, but it cannot build a green stem and leaves without light.

Why a Plant without Green Leaves becomes Sickly

Let us take a yellowish leaf from a plant grown in the dark, and a

1. The stem of the geranium has been severed and a piece of glass-tubing interposed.

Photos]   *[J. J. Ward.*
2. The same geranium fifteen days later. The flowers are still developing, but the leaves are deteriorating.

green leaf from a similar plant grown in the light. We then soak them both in boiling water until they become soft. After pouring off the water, place the leaves in a little methylated spirit. The leaves then soon become colourless, and the spirit changes to a green colour. Finally, remove the leaves from the spirit and paint them with the tincture of iodine you use should you cut your finger.

With the leaf grown in the dark, nothing happens, but the one grown in the light changes to a

13

brownish colour. The iodine is a test for starch, and the change of colour in the leaf exposed to the light shows that it contains starch grains ; while the one grown in the dark remains the same because it lacks starch.

A sickly plant with yellow leaves is, therefore, one that is dying from starvation—for starch is the food material it needs to make growth, and starch is formed only when the plant is exposed to light.

Also, the green colouring matter of the leaf, called "chlorophyll," which the methylated spirit dissolves out, can be developed only under the influence of sun-

Daffodil bulbs removed from a bowl, showing the roots seeking moisture by turning upwards into the atmosphere.

light. It is this green chlorophyll that absorbs the red and yellow rays of sunlight that are so much needed for starch formation. The green pigment is really a screen to reject the unwanted green rays, and it is these rejected rays that cause leaves to appear green to our eyes.

To Prove that Water is Forced up the Stem

Water is required in the leaf tissues, and has to be brought up from the soil after being absorbed by the roots. That a current of water is continually travelling up a plant stem may be shown by

Photos]   *[J. J. Ward.*
In the dark this seed potato could develop only a thin shoot bearing three tiny potatoes.

cutting through the stem of a geranium plant near the surface of the soil. Then interpose about three inches of glass-tubing, about the same thickness as the stem, connecting it with a bit of rubber tube. After filling it with water, join on the leaf-bearing stem with another ring of rubber tube, carefully avoiding air-bubble inclusion. Finally, add a supporting stick, and fasten with adhesive tape.

Now you have a plant stem connected with three inches of glass tubing through which all the water brought up by the roots must travel. Will the plant grow under those conditions ? A plant that was just about to flower, that I experimented with, not only continued to bloom, but even produced a second flowering branch three months later, although by that time the plant had become much weakened.

This experiment illustrates what is known as " root-pressure "—the force which keeps up the water supply, even to the topmost leaf on a great oak tree.

Even a cut flower, such as a white sweet pea, or a narcissus, if placed in a bottle of red ink, will soon show streaks

[*J. J. Ward.*

An epiphytal orchid whose roots suck moisture from the air.

of red colour in the veins of its petals. That, however, is not due to root-pressure, but is merely liquid diffusion.

Roots will penetrate to great depths in the soil in search of water. If a pot plant becomes too dry, its roots will sometimes come to the surface of the soil to seek moisture from the atmosphere. Bulbs often show their roots turned upwards.

HOW TO MAKE A CAMERA

ALL you need to make what is known as a pinhole camera is a small, well-made, light-proof box—such as a cigar box. Take out one of the sides, or a portion of one, and replace it with a thin sheet of metal, in the centre of which a very small opening, not larger than a pinhole, has been bored. If now you place a photographic plate against the side of the box facing the hole, you can obtain a good photograph which can be developed in the ordinary way. You should choose for your picture some stationary object, or a well-lit corner of the garden, because the rays of light entering the box through the tiny hole—which acts as a lens, are very feeble, and a long exposure (say of half an hour) is necessary. As focusing is impossible, one cannot determine definitely the amount of view included, and there will have to be a little guess-work. Our diagram illustrates a rough-and-ready method of getting over this difficulty. Make a central mark at the top back of the camera and mark out lines to each of the front corners Y Z. By looking along these lines, a rough idea of the view included can be gained.

This " pinhole " camera of yours is a development of the old Camera Obscura, which was a small, darkened building, in the roof of which was fixed a box containing a convex lens and a sloping mirror which reflected a view of the surrounding country on to a table in the centre.

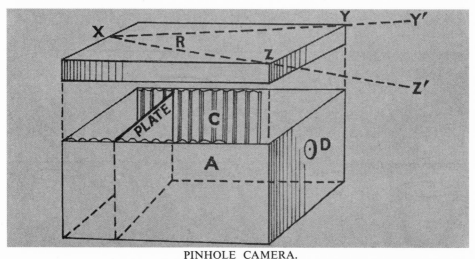

PINHOLE CAMERA.
A Box ; R, Close-fitting lid ; C, Corrugated paper to hold plate ; D, Pinhole.

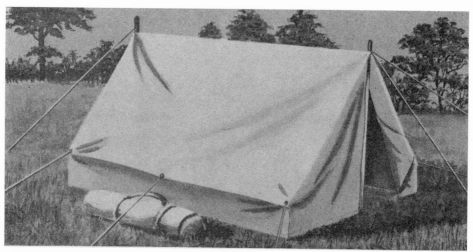

A USEFUL TYPE OF TENT, PORTABLE AND EASILY ERECTED.

CAMPING

FITTING out for camping in the open is a matter of discarding as much as possible rather than of taking everything that may be useful. Choose first the clothes that are least likely to suffer from getting wet, crumpled, or even slept in, and take only enough to last out the expedition. Don't put in a spare suit because it *may* be useful ; anything that merely *may* be useful should be left behind, and only the things that certainly will be wanted should be taken.

In regard to sleeping-kit, remember that overcoats will supplement blankets, as will other day clothing as well ; make use of these things when necessary, and thus save the carrying of blankets beyond what are really essential. Among the necessities will be a good ground sheet for each camper ; this is a cotton fabric sheet, about seven feet by four, rubbered on one side to make it waterproof ; any good firm of sports outfitters will supply such an article, and it serves a variety of uses besides that of keeping the damp from rising when one is sleeping. It makes a good waterproof in wet weather, draped round the shoulders ; a good holdall for sleeping kit when things are tidied up for the day, and may even be utilised as a washing bowl.

Be careful to see that the tent chosen, which must be a lightweight one, is large enough to contain all the occupants comfortably, and their belongings as well. Ventilation is one of the chief

HELPING WITH THE HAYMAKING. [*Sport & General.*

considerations. A closed tent is bound to become stuffy in wet weather, even if it is well-ventilated, while if the ventilation is defective it is not only unhealthy, but practically unbearable, with all its occupants in for any length of time.

Washing kit should be of the simplest. A canvas washing bowl, and, if away from facilities for bathing, a canvas bath as well, should be included, since enamelled or tin stuff renders packing a difficult matter. A handy bowl can be formed from a waterproof sheet either slung, or spread over a framework or basket.

What is to be taken in the way of cooking utensils is so much a matter of taste that it is difficult to advise. One kettle, one frying pan, and one saucepan, all preferably of aluminium, which is light and easy to clean, are essential. Knife, fork, and spoon must, of course, be carried. Some campers find that a piece of bread makes a plate that needs no washing up, while all should rule out crockery, if possible, and use aluminium plates and drinking vessels.

Remember, in pitching camp, that the meadow is not your property, and be most careful to fit in with the little prejudices of the person who has given permission for the camp to be pitched.

CAMPING

Thus, if there is a gate which is usually kept shut, make certain that that gate is properly shut after you have passed through it, for though the owner may forgive you for leaving the gate open, he will certainly like you better if you shut it. Again, every camp involves a certain amount of waste stuff during the day—paper and the like. See that this is all carefully collected and destroyed; and do not throw old tins away, but collect them for placing in a convenient dustbin, or for burial. The aim should be to leave the camping ground in just as good condition as when the site was chosen.

When it comes to the actual pitching of the tent, some little rise will be found even on the most level-looking ground, and this should be chosen as the site. Get your tent properly pitched on as high ground as possible, remembering that all water has to be carried; select your cooking place, if possible, so that it is sheltered from the prevailing wind, and place there such of the cooking materials and utensils as rain will not injure.

THE MORNING TUB.

[*Fox Photos.*

19

CAMPING

In regard to the cookhouse outfit, get four bricks, stand them on edge in two pairs, end to end, with just sufficient space between the pairs of bricks to admit of kettle and frying pan standing on them securely. This will be your cooking stove, and the bricks can be moved so that one of the open ends of the trench they form catches the wind that may be blowing at the time. Bricks are not always available, however, and a more reliable way of making a "grate" is to cut a trench, about four inches wide by a foot or so in length, turning back the excavated turf so that it forms a support for cooking pots.

Ample dry sticks for lighting a fire are usually easy to obtain, and it is wise, every night, to take inside the tent sufficient sere sticks for the lighting of the next morning's fire. Two or three

[*Sport & General.*

COOKING THE DINNER.

[*Fox Photos.*

ENJOYING A GAME OF LEAP-FROG.

" camp cookers," which are tins of solidified spirit, are useful things to include in the outfit ; they will save trouble in preparing a meal on a wet day, but should be regarded purely as emergency rations.

In wet weather, it will be found that heavy rain sends a light spray through the fabric of the tent for a minute or so, but after that the fibres of the fabric expand as they get soaked, and the tent becomes practically waterproof, although the fabric is wet on the inside. It is best not to touch that wet fabric in any way while the rain continues, as, with some materials, the touch is sufficient to cause water to collect at the spot touched instead of running down to the bottom of the fabric, and a steady drip inside the tent results. This may sometimes be cured by running a finger down the inside of the tent from top to bottom, but the cure is not always effective, and the fabric should be left untouched in any way until the tent is dry, or at least until the rain has stopped. Another thing to remember is that rain causes the guy ropes of a tent to shrink, with consequent extra pull on the pegs ; thus, as soon as possible, it is advisable to go round and see that all pegs are secure, and if necessary to reset any that have been pulled loose by the strain of the guy ropes, and to adjust the ropes themselves to a proper length. After rain, the " flies " of the tent should be taken off their pegs, and allowed to hang loose till dry, when they may be rolled and tied up for ventilating purposes. Guys should be slackened before turning in for the night, or the tent may collapse owing to dew shrinking the ropes.

If camping is to be a success, you must have some sort of discipline. Everyone must be allotted his share in the work, and times for rising, meals and bed must be settled and adhered to. Tidiness, especially in the tent, is essential. Beds should be carefully rolled up and, on fine days, put outside the tent to air.

SILHOUETTE PORTRAITS

CUTTING silhouettes of your friends forms an amusing occupation for a winter evening. Pin a large sheet of paper on the wall and sit the subject so that his shadow, of the right size, falls on the paper. Carefully sketch this outline and then cut the paper out.

MAKING A SILHOUETTE.

AN AEROPLANE OF PAPER

TAKE a square sheet of paper, and in turn fold edge *a* along each of the edges *b* to give the diagonal creases *c*. Fold the corners A up to the points B to produce the cross fold *d*, see

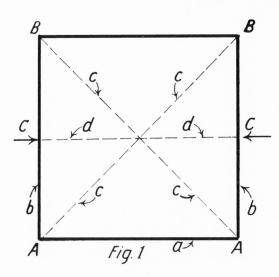

Figure 1, and open out the paper again. Then apply inward pressure at points C, while pinching together corners A on each side of creases *c*, and at the same time performing a similar pinching operation at corners B. The paper will then fold as in Figure 2, until, on flattening, it finally assumes the shape of Figure 3.

The next step is to fold down the front corners A to point D, the two halves of edge *a* meeting together down the centre line of the diamond so formed, giving Figure 4. Then, on the front flaps only, make the creases indicated by the dotted lines, by first folding edges *c* up to the centre line of the diamond, and then folding edges *f* down to the same centre line. Pinch together the corner portions *e* as shown in Figure 5, at the same time pressing down and forming the creases just made, into folds.

Fold the lower part backwards along the line *g-g* to produce the shape shown in Figure 6, the part E forming the body or fuselage, and F the wings of the aeroplane,

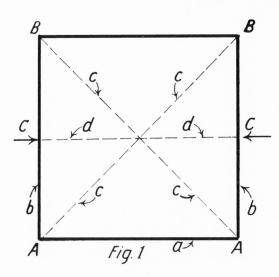 *Fig. 1*

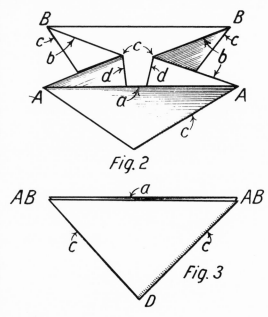 *Fig. 2*

Fig. 3

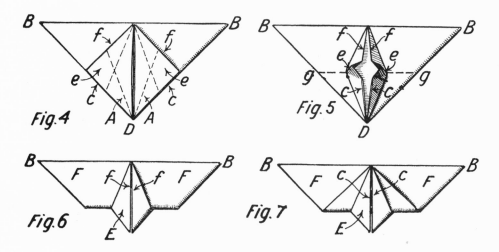

as seen from underneath. A view from above is shown in Figure 7. It is now necessary only to press the folds tightly and to give the wings a dihedral angle by bending them slightly upwards along the centre line of the body E.

A finish is given by adding a tail G, which is made by creasing a narrow strip of paper longitudinally and slipping it centrally between the under and upper surfaces of the wings, immediately below the body E. This tail not only improves the appearance but also improves the flying qualities. It is preferable to insert it into position at the stage shown in Figure 5, so that it becomes anchored in position by the folding which produces Figure 6. The finished aeroplane is shown in Figure 8, and it is best flown by grasping the tail at point H immediately behind the wings F, with the thumb and forefinger, and launching it sharply forward in a horizontal direction.

It can be made to do trick flying by bending the wing tips B up or down, and also by bending the end portion of the tail up or down across line *h*. The tail G can be made fast by means of a touch of gum or paste before it is inserted, if it is not held in position by the fold producing Figure 6.

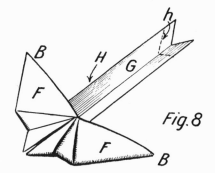

A BOY CHAMPION AND HIS TRAINER.

[*Fox Photos.*

IF YOU LIKE BOXING

ONE of the biggest problems which worry young boxers is—
should one start slow or fast? They hear that certain
champions are " slow starters," and they feel that perhaps the best
plan when getting up for the first round is to see what their opponent
can do while warming up.

More champions have been beaten through this negative policy
and slackness than is realised. The process of warming up merely
invites your opponent, just as strong as you are at the beginning,
to pile up points even if he cannot put you down.

The best defence is to attack, and from the moment you leave
your chair you should not allow your opponent to get into his
stride. In this way you keep him on the defensive and it is *you*
who will do the scoring.

Some boxers always look on the ground instead of at their
opponent's eyes. Is it better to watch your opponent's feet or try

to read what is in his mind from the expression in his eyes ? It is a matter of opinion, but most coaches will tell you that the eye betrays the mind more easily than the feet.

BAD HABITS

It is a bad fault to place too much reliance on ducking. Some young boxers make it such a habit that they simply invite an upper-cut as they rise. Duck to get out of trouble, but do not try it too often.

A fatal mistake is to push your opponent about. He will not object to your wasting your strength in this way—in fact, he will then lean on you so that you will just have to push him. Your best defence against this is to keep your man at a distance and hit him good and hard when he shows a tendency to try to take a rest on your shoulder.

Do not waste your stamina by swinging blows that never land. It is surprising how much energy is wasted on thin air.

Use your *brains* when you use your fists !

[*Topical Press.*

THE LAST ROUND OF THE " FINAL ".

A MODEL AERODROME.

HOW TO MAKE A MODEL AERODROME

THIS model aerodrome can be made whatever size you wish, according to the boxes you can find and also the amount of time you want to put into it. As your main part is the central control tower, I suggest that this should be started first. Grocers have many large boxes and if you approach them courteously in the matter, I am sure they will let you pick all the boxes you want.

Pick a good strong box for the lower central section, as this has to take quite a bit of weight. Get a box 14 inches by 14 inches and about 16 inches high. In order that you have a very realistic "run-through" for your motors when attending the air-port, cut out back and front doors 6 inches high and 6 inches wide. On each side have windows 3 inches high by 2 inches wide and above the doorways place windows 3 inches high and 4 inches wide. On each side of these put windows 3 inches high and 2 inches wide. Line these all with cellophane or waxed paper. If using the latter,

27

then you must line in the black strokes as shown in the sketch. Have no windows on the sides, at all. The measurements for both back and front will be the same, and the bottom of the box should be left intact to give strength.

The making of the balconies can be simplified by using large cardboard box lids inverted and placed on top of the lower boxes. Although you may have to add additional sections to these lids, you will at least have the firm foundation there.

The next step is to fit up the second and smaller part of the tower. You must use your judgment in getting your box for this. Choose one about 2 inches smaller than the lower one and certainly not so lofty. One about 8 inches high would be suitable. In this the windows should be 4 inches from the base of the box

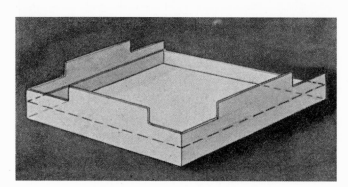

The facia boards fitted to the box.

in order to clear the balcony. Give these windows the modern round-the-corner trend. Make them 2 inches high and let them extend to 2 inches along the front and 3 inches along the sides. Carry the same idea out at the rear of the tower. If room permits, you can put in a long narrow window near to the top. This need only be 5 inches long and $1\frac{1}{2}$ inches high. Finish this off with another inverted box lid. Here again a separate facia board is planned in the illustration, together with a very modern clock.

The top tower storey can be as small as 9 inches square with a height of 8 inches. In all of these boxes I suggest leaving in the bottoms for additional strength. The top section would have just one long narrow window along the front and another along the back. Actually, it should go all round but would make the top insecure for the toy motor which must come on this. The top facia board can be deeper than the other two in order to cover up the motor turntable. Before fixing up any more of the model, we must consider the question of colouring. Being a modern building this

HOW TO MAKE A MODEL AERODROME

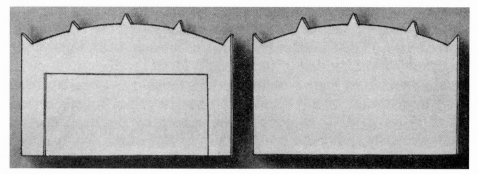

Front of the hangar.   Back of the hangar.

would not be red brick.   The most satisfactory material for getting a really attractive surface is a mixture of flat white paint, putty and sand.   Get a small tin of flat white paint to which add a lump of putty and some silver sand.   Allow this to stand for 48 hours, then put on with an old short-haired brush.   Dab it on, not too wet, but quite stodgy.   The facia boards should all be done white and the platforms all slate grey.

Meccano enthusiasts will already have the small turntable and will need little instruction in how to install this.   For those who have not got this little machine, it can be had for a few shillings. By fitting two wire stays out from the revolving section and making a neat hook on the ends, one can hang two miniature aeroplanes on these.   When the motor is set in motion, the planes then encircle the tower.

Illumination of the tower can be effected by putting small globes inside each box of the tower structure.

The making of the hangars can then be tackled and these can

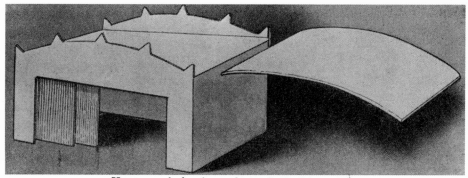

Hangar ready for the roofing to be fixed in position.

29

be made to whatever size you wish. As each hangar is made of a separate box, the aerodrome can be extended by the addition of more boxes. For several aerodromes I have used the strong "Anchor" Butter boxes. These are all 11 inches deep by 9 inches wide and 7 inches high. From the long sides cut a gap, 9 inches wide by 6 inches high. This will form the wide front entrance. There is no need to complicate the model by putting in other windows, as these would be unnecessary. Note the specially strong shapes shown in the illustrations which can be made up from strong cardboard and fixed on. These should have the small flaps as shown to take the roof. There is no need to take anything out of the back of the hangar, and this should remain entirely closed. All one has to do now is to make the roof by cutting a piece of cardboard to bend right over and overlap by about 1 inch. This should be painted with light grey paint and the hangars covered with slate-grey paper. Make the doors about 4 inches wide and just high enough to slide along inside the box. Fix a piece of " L "-shaped cardboard along the top of the box and about $\frac{1}{2}$ inch inside the doorway so that the doors slide along between these slots and the front of the hangar. Cover the doors with grained paper or paint them with flat red or grey paint.

No aerodrome would be complete without its Fire Station and Ambulance Depot. Small boxes about 5 inches by 7 inches by 5 inches high are useful for making these small detached buildings. Cut out windows in the sides 1 inch from the base and about $1\frac{1}{2}$ inches high by 2 inches long. In the short end cut doors 4 inches wide and 4 inches high. These buildings can be used for other additions.

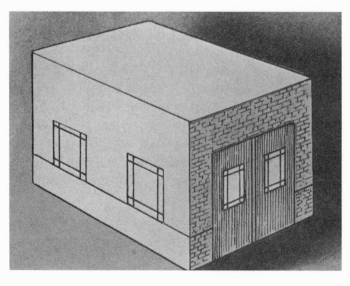

Fire Station Ambulance Depot.

SWALLOWS.

OUT-OF-DOORS. I

WHAT TO LOOK FOR IN SPRING

IF you know what to look for and where to look for it, you will
see more in a mile-long walk than most people will find in a
five-mile tramp. It does not matter whether you live in town or
country, for even a park or open space near a large city is full of
interest for those who have eyes to see.

Nature provides us with an abundance of sights all the year
round, and some of the most wonderful happenings in the world go
on close to our doorsteps, often in our gardens.

For our spring walks we will take the months of March, April
and May, although for some of Dame Nature's creatures spring
commenced earlier than February ! The raven, for instance, largest
and one of the rarest members of our crow family, commenced
repairing its great nest in January, up among the wilder hills of Wales
and along the rocky western coasts. Nearer at home bird song is
increasing, and we may, in mild weather, hear the song thrush,
blackbird, skylark, and the calls of the tit family before March has
arrived.

Spring is, of course, the great time when our summer visitors

31

arrive from Africa, Asia, and even from farther afield. About thirty different kinds of birds reach our shores between the end of March and the beginning of May, and spread in waves all over these islands. If you keep a notebook, you will find it very interesting to write down the dates on which you first saw or heard them, as this varies each year according to the weather.

Earliest of all migrants is the wheatear, to be seen on open spaces and moorland about March 28th. It is a little larger than a robin, has a white throat, black wings and black and white tail, and flies with a dipping movement among the boulders and gorse bushes with a call of "chack, chack." A little fellow, very difficult to see because he is continually on the move among the bare branches, comes soon after, and you will hear his signature tune of "chiff, chaff, chevvy, chif, chaf" long before you actually find him. It is, of course, the chiff-chaff, our earliest warbler, olive green in colour, and very common wherever there are plenty of trees and undergrowth.

Cuckoo.

Raven.

Close on the chiff-chaff's heels comes another warbler, very hard to distinguish from its cousin except by the song, which is a sweet musical trill gradually going down the scale. This is the song of the willow warbler, another lover of trees.

The sand martin is the first of the

Skylark.

32

Goat Willow.

swallow tribe, and his brown plumage will distinguish him from the house martin, which soon follows. The true swallow comes about mid-April, and may be known by the very long tail with needle-like feathers, and the darker plumage. We all know and love the cuckoo, arriving during the third week in April, and the swift with its screaming cry. But did you know that the cuckoo does not open its beak to make the familiar call, and that the swift is not related to the swallow, but to the nightjar, a bird which loves bracken tracts in the woods ?

Insects, too, are answering the call of spring, and if we look carefully on the northern sides of willow trees, we may find the beautiful puss moth newly emerged from its hard cocoon, which was glued to the bark all the winter. Empty snail-shells do not seem very interesting objects, but often a deserted home contains a mason bee, which has made its home there, sealing itself up from August until April.

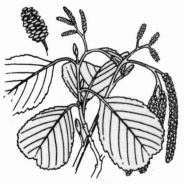

Alder Catkin.

Coltsfoot is the first wild plant to flower, and its golden-yellow heads will be found in many waste places. Notice how the heads droop down to prevent the cold rain from entering the flowers, each of which may produce 20,000 seeds !

The "lamb's tails," or hazel catkins, are very familiar sights in spring, but there are far more interesting ones to be found. The sallow catkins are lovely with their yellow " dust," and the white poplar bears a pretty, feathery bloom. The walnut tree has large catkins, and the streamside alder is thick with another kind.

Birds will be nesting all through

Hazel Nuts and Catkins.

COAL TITMOUSE.

Nightjar.

these spring months, and many a beautiful clutch of eggs can be seen in nests on the ground, in the hedgerow and bank, up in the trees, and by the water-side. Naturalists and those who are fortunate enough to possess a good book on British birds will not find much difficulty in recognising the eggs of different birds. For instance, those of the tits are usually white, spotted with light red ; those of the wheatear, greenish-blue, faintly speckled with rust-red ; those of the chiff-chaff, white, spotted purplish-brown with violet-grey underlying blotches ; those of the skylark, dull-buffish-white, varying to pale olive, densely mottled with greyish-brown ; all are as easily recognised as the actual bird, by the expert. Do not disturb the nests, for some of those nests took many days of patient building. The long-tailed tit's nest often contains two thousand feathers ! A collection of eggs is merely a box of empty shells, but the living bird is charming at all times, and during the spring most of them consume enormous numbers of harmful insects, caterpillars and other pests.

Blue Tit and Great Tit.

CRESTED TITMOUSE.

WHEATEAR.

SOME INDOOR GAMES—
WITH PENCIL AND PAPER

OUR TED

EVERY blank in the following passage is to be filled with a word ending in the syllable -*ted*.

Ted was a very nice boy, and therefore (1) —— quite a lot of friends. He had charming manners, a well (2) —— voice, and when describing his experiences became quite (3) —— and enthusiastic. When his special friend (4) —— a Swiss holiday, he was (5) —— at the prospect, and from then onward (6) —— much thought to the question of saving the necessary money. A little was set aside weekly and this soon (7) —— up. The holiday was a great success, and although the weather became unsettled, and wet periods (8) —— with sunny ones, nothing (9) —— from the beauty that surrounded Ted and his companion on every side. One climb was rendered memorable by the fact that the heat was so great that they were almost (10) ——, but they were determined not to be (11) —— from reaching the summit of the mountain, so they (12) —— in their efforts, until their attention was (13) —— by threatening clouds. Rain began to fall heavily, and although they (14) —— the idea of getting drenched to the skin, they were not (15) ——. On they went, and finally gained their objective. By this time the clouds had (16) —— and below them was an awe-inspiring panorama. Ted's eyes (17) —— with wonder and he (18) —— with joy. His friend, on the other hand, sat and (19) —— on the glory of the scene. Both were supremely (20) ——

Solutions

1. Attracted	8. Alternated	15. Daunted
2. Modulated	9. Detracted	16. Drifted
3. Animated	10. Prostrated	17. Dilated
4. Suggested	11. Prevented	18. Shouted
5. Elated	12. Persisted	19. Ruminated
6. Devoted	13. Diverted	20. Contented.
7. Mounted	14. Hated	

INDOOR GAMES

ANIMALS IN HIDING

The name of one or two animals is concealed in each numbered sentence, the letters of the name being used in the correct order and in sequence. Total number of animals is seventeen.

Solutions

1. The grass had been trampled, but he found a perfect dandelion standing erect.
   Ass, ape, lion
2. He entered the cathedral.
   Cat
3. Fear dogs me, and I still am beaten sometimes.
   Dog, lamb
4. His eye lighted on keys that had been left behind on a seat
   Donkey
5. Tom, are you coming ? The train will go at six o'clock
   Mare, goat
6. I am ill. Call Hannah, or send for a doctor.
   Horse
7. You will never be a real force if you are so easily cowed
   Bear, cow
8. He seemed to be worrying, or ill at ease, and just a tap irritated him, though it was in fun.
   Gorilla, tapir
9. You and Dinah are quite right ; if you cannot transfer, return the tickets.
   Hare, ferret
10. The paths were like a maze, branching out in all directions.
    Zebra.

CONCEALED TOWNS

The names of towns in the British Isles, twenty in all, are hidden in the following passage. They may be a word, part of a word, or part of several, the letters of the name again being used in the correct order and in sequence. (Example : '' His father bought him a new bat, heavy and strong ''—*Bath*.)

Solutions

I had been reading about a new market place which had been built in a town a few miles away, so decided that I would go to see it. I told my brother Arthur so, and, as he liked my idea, let him come along too. Our way lay along a straight road and over a hill, then round a great ring of trees. We had not been near the wood for days ; we found we had to get over a pool, easy enough to jump, but when we

Reading
Newmarket

Thurso, Deal
Andover
Tring
Woodford
Poole

were across it we saw, to our alarm, a large snake.   Ross

"O, bang it with your stick, Arthur," I shouted.   Oban
He gave it several blows, and it rolled over, but I was   Dover
not satisfied.

"Give it another bang, or it will recover and be   Bangor
ready to frighten someone else. We must beware of   Ware
that spot in future," I said as we continued our
journey. "If Mary or Kate had been with us they   York
would have been terrified, and as for Mother, well,   Motherwell
I can't imagine what she would have done."

"She would not have come with us in any case,"
said Arthur, "for she relies a great deal on Donald   Shere
nowadays, and prefers to go in the car with him."   London

The air was fresh and a real tonic as we trudged   Alton
along ; the sky looked bright, on ahead of us, and we   Brighton
soon recovered from every fear.   Frome.

BODY BUILDING

The solutions are all parts of the human body.

		Solutions
1.	Employees	Hands
2.	Two tall trees	Palms
3.	Receptacle	Chest
4.	Ammunition	Arms
5.	Holiday requisite	Trunk
6.	Shell-fish	Muscles
7.	Salt-water fish	Soles
8.	Ships	(Blood) vessels
9.	A deer	Heart
10.	Found in marble	Veins
11.	Two berries	Hips
12.	Extravagance	Waist
13.	What a plumber has to deal with	Joints
14.	A measurement	Foot
15.	Parts of a chair	Legs
16.	Two young animals	Calves
17.	Sacred building	Temple
18.	Most buildings have one of these	Roof
19.	Musical instrument used in jazz band	Drum

INDOOR GAMES

BODY BUILDING (*continued*)

20.	Fruit	Adam's apple
21.	Scholars	Pupils
22.	Personal pronoun	Eye
23.	A cover	Lid
24.	Used to cross a river	Bridge
25.	Negatives	Nose
26.	Part of a hill	Brow
27.	Boat propeller	Skull
28.	Part of a saw	Teeth.

OLD NURSERY RHYMES

The answer to each statement is the title of a Nursery Rhyme.

1.	One who was lazy and neglected the call to duty	Little Boy Blue
2.	A sad climbing fatality	Jack and Jill
3.	A journey to town to see a much decorated lady accompanied by music	Ride-a-cock Horse
4.	Story of a young lady who got only as much as she worked for	See Saw Marjory Daw
5.	A case of overcrowding and parental neglect	There was an old woman
6.	One of nervous temperament who, whilst partaking of light refreshment, was rudely interrupted	Little Miss Muffet
7.	One whose sedentary occupation was suddenly cut short by an accident	Humpty Dumpty
8.	One who insisted on doing his own courting	A Frog who would
9.	One who at a festive season exhibited an unwarranted pride in his own virtue	Little Jack Horner
10.	A genial old gentleman with decidedly musical taste	Old King Cole
11.	A sad tale of poverty and a kind-hearted old soul	Old Mother Hubbard.

MAKING MANY WORDS FROM ONE

The object is to make as many words as possible from a chosen word. Two-letter words should be ignored, and only the actual letters in the selected word must be used ; that is to say, if *a* appears once in the word, it must not be used more than once in any of the words that are made.

A suitable word would be one like " Comradeship," and it will be a surprise to those who have not tried this game to find what a large number of words can be extracted. After a " trial trip " a system will be evolved, and there will be a hectic rush to write as many words as possible in the given time. Five minutes should be allowed.

The players then total their words. Another method of scoring is for the players to read their lists in turn whilst the others strike out all the duplicates they have. Each player then scores according to the number of words on his list that have been thought of by no one else.

A SWARM OF ANTS

The solutions are all words ending in the syllable *-ant*.

	Solutions
1. A waiting ant	Attendant
2. A floating ant	Buoyant
3. A plentiful ant	Abundant
4. A hard ant	Adamant
5. A needy ant	Want
6. A noisy ant	Blatant
7. A graceful ant	Elegant
8. An enormous ant	Elephant
9. A shirking ant	Truant
10. A wandering ant	Vagrant
11. A disinfecting ant	Deodorant
12. A servile ant	Sycophant
13. A vacillating ant	Hesitant
14. A dunce-like ant	Ignorant
15. An ant on the look-out	Expectant
16. A light-giving ant	Luminant
17. A sweet-smelling ant	Fragrant
18. A helpful ant	Assistant
19. An ant of consequence	Important
20. A domestic ant	Servant

A SWARM OF ANTS (*continued*)

	Solutions
21. A growing ant	Plant
22. A learned and precise ant	Pedant
23. An ambitious ant	Aspirant
24. A coming-in ant	Entrant
25. A meagre ant	Scant
26. An unceasing ant	Incessant
27. A residential ant	Tenant
28. A despotic ant	Tyrant
29. A ticklish ant	Irritant
30. A journeying ant	Itinerant
31. A joyous ant	Jubilant
32. A sloping ant	Slant
33. A shining ant	Brilliant
34. A brawling ant	Termagant
35. A web-footed ant	Cormorant
36. A humbugging ant	Cant
37. A singing ant	Chant
38. A green ant	Verdant
39. A talkative ant	Conversant
40. A measuring ant	Sextant
41. A hanging ant	Pendant
42. A fighting ant	Assailant
43. An entreating ant	Supplicant
44. A gasping ant	Pant
45. A bestowing ant	Grant
46. A pleasing ant	Pleasant

MISSING ADJECTIVES

To prepare this game take a passage from a book or newspaper. Strike out a dozen of the adjectives. Then dictate the passage to the players, saying " blank " when you come to the adjectives.

There are two ways of finishing off the game : (*a*) Leave players to fill in the blanks with what they consider the most suitable adjectives, and then read out the correct ones, for checking. (*b*) Give them the list of adjectives, but in a different order, and let them fill them in where they ought to go, in a given space of time.

A SPECTACULAR "SAVE."

FOOTBALL, A MOST POPULAR SPORT

SOCCER

A GOOD footballer never misses an opportunity of seeing other and better men play. He learns a great deal from them, and that is why you should give quite ten per cent of your spare time to watching the best professionals and the best amateurs. Between the two schools of soccer there is a vast deal of difference, yet both can teach you much, and in this article are a number of points which you are sure to notice if you are observant in a football sense.

WING PLAY

Watch how the class winger, in receiving a pass, allows the ball to come to him at the moment when he is actually *on the run*. There is no stopping the ball first, pushing it forward, and then setting off for goal or along the touchline. He is in his stride and running fast when he meets the ball. It is surprising how many

[*Fox Photos.*

A CLEVER "SAVE" DURING AN IRISH-WELSH SCHOOLBOY INTERNATIONAL.

valuable seconds may be saved in this way, and a spread-eagled defence given no time to recover.

You will see how a good wing forward tries to obtain a corner for his side. He will race the ball down the wing and then, hearing a back chasing him, will suddenly stop short and side-step. The back, unable to pull up, goes over the line, taking the ball with him and registering a corner for his opponents.

On the other hand, a good back, let it be said, watches points such as these. As he races up alongside, a judicious short charge will put the winger off the ball and cause it to trickle over the line for a goal-kick, thus relieving what might have been a dangerous situation.

There are wingers who *never* use their brains. If you have to play in this position, do not bemoan your fate if the pass you desire never comes. First of all, your defence may be so overrun that they haven't the time to get the ball to you. Similarly, your inside man may be helping the defence.

Then again, a good back will position himself between you and your players so that any pass that comes across is immediately intercepted and sent back. It is up to you in such circumstances to wander. Go inside ! Then, suddenly, you will receive a pass and the back will find you are not where he expected you to be. *You must help where your men cannot help you.*

Even the centre-forward should try to get the ball sometimes instead of standing idly by, waiting for the pass that never seems to arrive. More especially is this so when he is up against a tall, clever centre-half who loves shadowing him all over the field.

It is a common occurrence for young players—and indeed, quite good-class amateurs—to carry on a long battle on the touchline before the ball either goes out of play or is returned well into the field. Watch the professional or the international amateur. He has not the slightest compunction about kicking the ball out when

[*Central Press.*

MID-FIELD PLAY.

necessary. You must remember that this is not unsportsmanlike—it is the game. By putting the ball out, a wing half, for example, allows his backs to re-position themselves, whereas he might lose the ball to the opposing centre-forward or inside man, who would at once make tracks for goal.

THIS IMPORTANT DEFENDER

Watch a first-class goalkeeper receive a ball. He sees that his body is always behind it, so as to form a barrier if the ball should slip out of his hands. If he takes the ball on the ground he may go down on one knee. It is often fatal merely to *bend* down. The ball will be slippery if the weather is bad, and can so quickly cannon off his hands, strike a foot, and go into the goal at a tangent. By dropping down on one knee the body is still behind the ball.

A good goalkeeper will never make a spectacular save if he can avoid it. This type of save is often resorted to by the famous Continental goalkeepers. Admittedly it looks a brilliant piece of work from the spectators' point of view, but a goalkeeper lying on the ground is the backs' biggest worry. He is useless until he is once more between the goal-posts. The world's greatest goal-keepers always make the best saves seem simple—and the secret is clever anticipation of what the opponent is going to do with the ball.

To young goalkeepers here is a special word of advice. *Please* take all goal-kicks yourselves, no matter how many there may be. Obviously, the more you get in a match the more certain it is that your backs are having a hard afternoon. Their job is gruelling enough without needing to do some of your work, too !

There are some inexperienced goalkeepers who have one big failing—they will not get rid of the ball. They carry it and, harried, seem unable to clear. The result is that goal area scrimmages are far too frequent, and these cause the other defenders much anxiety and trouble. If you are a goalkeeper, make it a rule to rid yourself of the ball at the first possible opportunity.

A word to goalkeepers, too, about the long, punted shot on a gusty afternoon which is so deceiving and often scores silly goals. A back, for instance, will take a blinder. The ball sails up on the wind and drops somewhere about the penalty area. The goal-keeper, unthinking, rushes out and the ball, hesitating or seeming to, gracefully bounces over his head. He then has the mortification of racing madly back but without a chance in a million of stopping the ball entering the net. Stay in goal for shots such as these! This is a hint you simply must learn.

Because a goalkeeper cannot afford to make mistakes, here is another piece of advice, given to the writer by a famous International goalkeeper. You should always receive corner kicks by placing yourself at the end of the goal farthest from the incoming shot. The reason is that it is easier to run *forward* and punch clear than to try to recover as the ball sails overhead.

He also said that unscrupulous opponents will often station one man half-way up the goal, so that the goalkeeper cannot cover the whole of his charge. This unfairness can be overcome, however, by one of the backs placing that man offside—a dangerous procedure because the referee might be unsighted—or by the other back stationing himself in front of the forward and so spoiling *his* view.

[Fox Photos.

LEARNING HOW TO TACKLE.

FOOTBALL

CLEVER BACKING-UP

Notice how good half-backs and backs will never admit defeat. A forward, let us say, is tackled by the half-back and wins through. On goes the player towards the back. The half, instead of chasing the player and perhaps getting in the way of the back, runs *behind* the back, so that, should the back be beaten, he is ready once again to take up the defence of the goal. Similarly, a beaten back will sometimes run behind his goalkeeper or post himself so that he can intercept a pass. Defensive craftiness is a great asset.

Notice how the best defenders never waste time. A back will kick cleanly down the field towards one of his own men. He will certainly not dribble, and perhaps lose the ball. Hundreds of goals in junior football have been lost because a back " messed about " instead of doing his job.

You may find when watching the experts that there are backs adept at playing the offside game—placing the opposing players

[Fox Photo

CAPTURING THE BALL.

offside. While this is very amusing to watch, and quite a legitimate manœuvre, it can be broken down if only the forwards will watch what they are doing. If any one of the five forwards lies too far up-field, it is certainly easy for the backs to walk three paces forward and so earn a free kick !

But what a chance there is when the centre, awaiting his opportunity, pushes the ball between the backs and runs for it ! Then *they* are in trouble. The offside game should be looked upon as defensive weakness. Don't play it !

[Fox Photos.

A NARROW MISS.

GENERAL HINTS

Keep the ball low no matter what your position may be. This is the best Scottish style of football. If you punt the ball into the air you are merely allowing your opponents to take up defensive or attacking positions.

An unwritten law of football is—short pass on hard ground, long pass when the going is soft. The reason for this is fairly obvious ; but how often is it forgotten ! With the ground a sea of mud and the ball heavy as lead, it is quite impossible to find one another by short passing. Resolute defenders will merely dash between as the ball slows up, and crash it out of harm's way. While short passing is usually resorted to on hard ground, there is no reason why it should not be mixed with long passing ; for it must always be remembered that the more you sling the ball about, the easier it should be to open up the defence.

MAGIC NUMBER NINE

WHEN the figures resulting from the multiplication of nine by each figure from two to twenty are added together the number nine results in each case :—

e.g. $2 \times 9 = 18$, i.e. $1 + 8 = 9$. $3 \times 9 = 27$, i.e. $2 + 7 = 9$. $20 \times 9 = 180$, i.e. $1 + 8 + 0 = 9$.

Choose any given number and reverse the order of the figures, then subtract the smaller number from the greater. The difference is always divisible by nine without a remainder, e.g. :—

$$678425$$
$$524876$$
$$\overline{}$$
$$9)153549$$
$$\overline{}$$
$$17061$$

If a much bigger number, running into millions is taken, the result is still the same, e.g. :—

$$684,107,233$$
$$332,701,486$$
$$\overline{}$$
$$9)351,405,747$$
$$\overline{}$$
$$39,045,083$$

If only three figures are used, the result is the same, and the quotient will always read backwards and forwards the same, e.g. :—

$$864$$
$$468$$
$$\overline{}$$
$$9)396$$
$$\overline{}$$
$$44$$
$$\overline{}$$

HOW TO USE A PANTOGRAPH

A PANTOGRAPH makes it possible to redraw accurately on a different scale maps and drawings merely by running a stencil over the original. The construction of such an instrument is almost as simple as its use ; the accompanying diagram gives all needful information. The pantograph being an instrument, however, its parts must work smoothly and regularly, and its simplicity of construction must not be an excuse for slovenly work. It is important to bear in mind that, whatever the scale of the pantograph, the distance from A to B must always equal that from C to E,

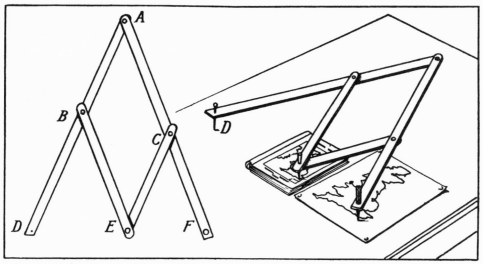

How a pantograph is used.

similarly BE must equal CA. When in use the pantograph is anchored to the drawing board or table at D ; this may be done by a long drawing pin, as shown, but it is generally advisable to supplement this by a weight of some sort, as upon the security of this corner, and the smooth working of the joints, depends the absence of " jump " on the part of the drawing pencil. The scale of the enlargement is decided by the relative positions of the movable points E and F and the pivot point D. If the tracing pencil, or stencil, at E is then carefully drawn over the original it will be found that the pencil at F will accurately reproduce the drawing on a larger scale. By changing the positions of E and F reproductions can be made on a *reduced* scale.

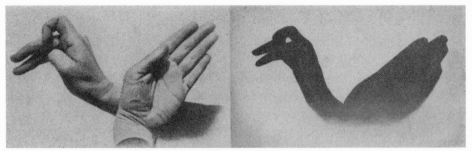
The Swan.

SHADOW SILHOUETTES

To become really expert in making shadow silhouettes considerable time must be spent in practice, in order to learn how to secure the best positions.

A few subjects are illustrated here, and a little experience with these will soon enable the performer to invent many other equally good ones —especially if he uses a few card-

The Rabbit.

board figures, which may be easily made. The Swan and the Rabbit are quite easy and quickly mastered, but figures like that of the Dustman and his pipe and the Clergyman on the next page, require quite a lot of patience and practice before they should be attempted in public.

The Helmet, shown below, is one of the easiest of silhouettes,

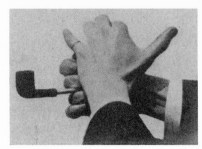

The Dustman and his pipe.

SHADOW SILHOUETTES

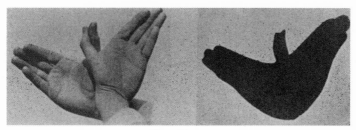

The Helmet.

and another very easy one is that of a dog's head with the mouth open or closed. This, almost every boy and girl knows how to make. It is an adaptation of the Swan's Head on page 233. You simply hold the right hand in front of the screen, fingers straight out, thumb pointing upwards to form the dog's ear, first finger doubled back to form the top of the dog's head and eye, the remaining fingers quite naturally form the nose and mouth. If the little finger is moved slowly up and down, the effect of opening and closing the mouth is realistically produced. A little manipulation and practice in the placing of the first finger when folded back will enable you to obtain the dog's eye, shown as a spot of light. Needless to say, the silhouette is easily recognisable as that of a Greyhound.

A candle will supply sufficient lighting if the room is reasonably small. The hands should be held about two feet away from the candle, and about four feet away from the screen, which should be tightly stretched on a wooden frame. It is best to work with the screen supported on the edge of a table, the scenery and arms can then be rested on the table if necessary, though very often the scenery is fixed in the sides of the frame. Considerable fun may be had from this pastime if sham fights and the like are introduced.

The Clergyman.

53

THE STRING AND BUTTON
PUZZLE

AN interesting little puzzle may be made from a sheet of stiff paper, a length of string, and two buttons, as shown in the illustration on this page.

In the sheet of paper are cut two parallel slits, a, $\frac{1}{4}$ of an inch apart and below the slits is cut a circular hole, b, $\frac{3}{8}$ of an inch in diameter. Through the hole b is passed a string c, which is passed through the two slits a as shown, and to the ends of the string are fastened two buttons d.

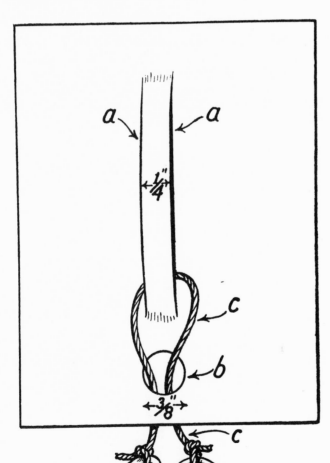

The puzzle consists in removing the string from the paper without tearing the paper in any way, or forcing the buttons d through the hole b so as to tear the paper.

As to how the puzzle is done, the secret lies in pulling the strip of paper lying between the slits a forward into a loop and passing it through the hole b, and this permits of the string c and one of the buttons d being easily unthreaded.

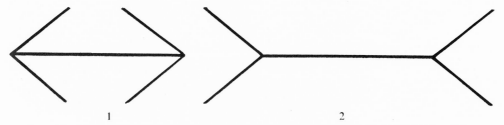

Which has the longer centre line, the figure on the left or the right ?

IS SEEING BELIEVING ?—I

MOST of you know the old saying that seeing is believing ; but this is not by any means always true. The fact of the matter is that, because you think you see a thing, it does not by any means always follow that it is as you think. Wonderful as the human eye undoubtedly is in its construction, it has its faults and limitations, and these cause it at times to deceive us over the most simple matters.

The judging of distance is not so easy as one might think. Here is a simple test for you. Which is the longer centre line in the above diagram, 1 or 2 ? Of course you will say 2 immediately, but you will be wrong for the horizontal lines are exactly the same length. This illusion is purely due to the introduction of the arrowheads, which in one case point inwards and in the other outwards.

The mistakes of the eye have to be taken into account by architects and builders. Evidently, the ancient Romans had studied these illusions, for on the fresco paintings of Pompeii are lines which should be parallel and are not parallel when measured mathematically, but are bent so as to compensate for the effect of adjacent lines. " Perspective," which every artist learns early in his career, is another illusion. It means that parallel lines going towards the horizon appear to meet and have to be drawn so that, if produced, they would meet at a distant point. This is necessary because, as you may know, the eye judges distances by comparing one eye's view with the other, and the farther away a spot is from the eye, the nearer together are the lines of vision from the two eyes.

Oblique lines always have a disturbing effect on our sense of direction. An instance of this form of illusion is illustrated on the next page ; the four perpendicular rules are perfectly straight and of even width, although, at a first glance, they do not appear to be so. Their straightness may be tested by means of laying a ruler along them.

Yet another example of the effect of oblique lines is shown in the next diagram, where the diagonal lines are all perfectly straight and parallel in spite of their irregular appearance. Test them with the ruler and see.

In another diagram is shown the strange effect produced by placing a straight rule on a background of curved lines. The rule appears to bend downwards at the ends in the

Look at this example of the effect of oblique lines. The diagonal lines are perfectly straight.

opposite direction to that followed by the curved lines. Actually, of course, the rule is quite straight. A variation of this illusion may be obtained by drawing an equilateral triangle on a background of circles. The sides of the triangle, although perfectly straight, will appear to bend inwards in the centres.

In another of our diagrams on the next page is shown the curious effect produced by a series of closely and widely spaced parallel lines, or shading, upon a centre band made up of evenly spaced parallel lines. The closely spaced lines, or dark shading clearly tends to lighten up the centre strip and make the parallel lines appear wider apart, whereas the widely spaced lines have the opposite effect.

The eye is very bad at comparing perpendicular and horizontal lines. If you draw on a piece of paper a thick horizontal line and then extend from the middle of it a perpendicular line of exactly the same length, you will find that your first impression is that the horizontal line

The four perpendicular rules are of even width and perfectly straight.

is much shorter than the other.

Now look at the three squares illustrated on

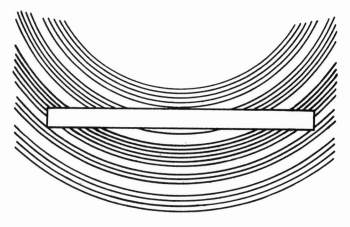

Here we have a straight rule on a background of curves—does it appear straight ?

page 58. In spite of the fact that they are all exactly the same size, they look entirely different and the square composed of horizontal lines here looks bigger than the square composed of the same number of perpendicular lines.

If you look at an electric lamp when it is alight, you will be able to see the filament quite easily. It looks quite a thick piece of wire, but examine it when it is cool and you will find that in reality the wire is most finely drawn. The difference is not due to expansion of the wire, which is too small to be observed, but simply to the fact that the bright object makes a stronger impression. Actually the wire does not change in size at all. It only appears to do so.

The eye is always eager to make comparisons, and for this reason a divided line always looks longer than one which is not divided. This is clearly illustrated in the diagrams on page 59.

The direct perception of the several parts makes us notice the number of the subdivisions, the size of which is more perceptible than when the parts are not marked off.

There are other things which appear to change places, even while we look at them, although they do not really alter their positions at

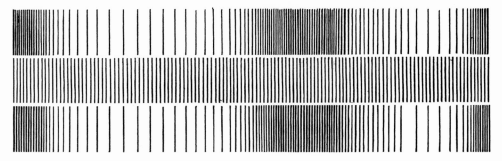

A curious effect produced by parallel lines.

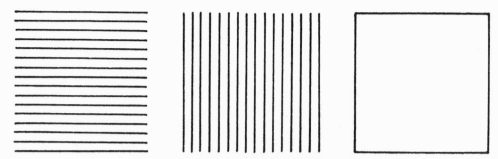

Can you say which of these squares is the largest ?

all. Our eyes are merely playing tricks with us. Look at our first diagram of a batch of cubes and say how many cubes you see. You will most probably see seven complete cubes. Now look at the first set of three cubes illustrated on the next page and then back at the larger group and count the cubes again. There are now only six, apparently, but a glance at the second group of three on the next page and then back at the large group again quickly restores the missing cube. And now as you look at the cubes in the first figure, they seem to change backwards and forwards of their own accord, first there are six and then seven.

Another form of this apparent rapid change may be seen in the case of the next two diagrams. Look at the first and you will have no hesitation in saying that the black wall is nearest you, and that the staircase mounts upwards. But if you look steadily at the lower figure for a moment or two and then back at the top one, you will instantly change your mind. It is now clear that the white wall is nearer to you and the staircase is inverted. And it appears to change from one to the other while you gaze at it.

Here is an interesting experiment that demonstrates the fact that light is only

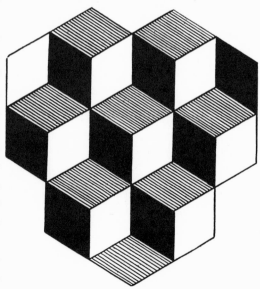

Now, how many cubes are there here ?

IS SEEING BELIEVING ?

A line that is broken up invariably looks longer than one which is not.

Here is another example of this.

made evident, as far as the eye is concerned, when it is scattered or changed in direction. Prepare a disc of glass of similar size to a penny. Have this disc concealed in a pocket then place a handkerchief over a penny and hold it over a glass full of water. By putting the hand to the pocket, ostensibly for a pencil with which the penny is tapped to show that it is still under the handkerchief, the glass disc can be substituted.

If this imitation penny is then dropped into the tumbler and the handkerchief removed, the sound is heard but the glass remains invisible and the penny can be said to have dissolved.

When the water is poured out, surface attraction prevents the glass disc from falling away.

Here is an optical illusion with a ring. Suspend a ring by a string, on a level with the eyes, with the plane of the ring towards the person. Tie a small stick crosswise on the end of another about a yard long ; hold the long stick, shut one eye, and try to thread the ring with the crossed stick. Success is not likely to be attained, but if both eyes are used, the ring can be threaded at the first attempt.

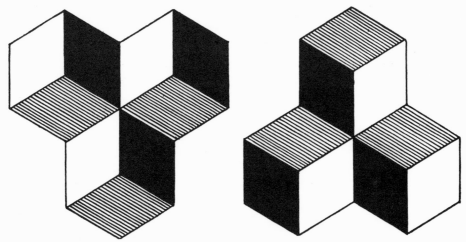

Compare these figures with the cubes on page 58.

59

IS SEEING BELIEVING ?

This trick may be varied by using only a crooked stick instead of two sticks tied crosswise.

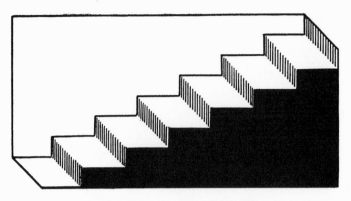

Is the black wall the nearer or the white one ?

The following is an illusion that will cause great surprise. Put a shilling into an ordinary tumbler half full of water ; place a plate on the top, and turn the glass over quickly, so that the water does not escape. On the plate a coin the size of half-a-crown will appear, and a little higher up another the size of a shilling. It will add to the effect of the experiment if one who does not know the trick is requested to throw the water away, and save the pieces. He will be surprised at finding only one.

Here is an illusion that you can make for yourself. Cut out a piece of white card—postcard will do, $2\frac{3}{8}$ inches by $1\frac{1}{4}$ inches and divide it up with a pencil into $\frac{1}{2}$-inch squares with an $\frac{1}{8}$th of an inch space between each. This should give you twelve $\frac{1}{2}$-inch squares with spaces between. Now black the squares in, but be careful to leave the narrow spaces between white. Fix your eyes on the black squares and in a few moments you will notice small shadowy dark dots appearing in the centres of all the white space crossings. Of course, these shadowy dots are not there at all really, and immediately you concentrate your gaze upon any one of them it disappears. It is only your eyes that are playing tricks.

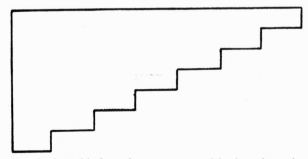

Now look at this for a few moments and back again at the top diagram.

WATCHING AN EXPERT.　　　　　　　[*Fox Photos.*

BETTER HOCKEY

THE most exciting position on the hockey field is undoubtedly that of centre-forward. He or she gets the opportunity of making spectacular shots at goal ; he or she is able to send over those long passes which so often lead to goals ; he or she is the one who holds the front line together.

Centre-forward play, however, calls for certain qualities. You must be a fast sprinter ; you must be able to shoot without stopping the ball first ; you must have a good eye. A slow centre-forward would cause a goalkeeper intense joy, because he or she would be able to take up position and save most of the shots.

If you are not cut out for centre-forward, have you the attributes of a good back ? Here " safety first " is much more important than brilliance. You must be good at interpreting what the attacker is going to do with the ball. As with the centre-

61

forward, however, you must be able to hit the ball without stopping it first, quickly sending it onwards. And you cannot afford to miss it—that would be fatal. Coolness under pressure and a capacity for never ceasing to worry an opponent are necessary for all hockey backs.

Would you like to be a goalkeeper? This is a thankless task. Every mistake may mean a goal. But, on the other hand, a really good goalkeeper is a match-winner to any side. First you want a good eye. The best goalkeepers seldom leave their charge. When they do, however, they always see that they obstruct the vision of the attacker.

To leave a wide open space is just what the attacking player is looking for.

No matter what your position is on the field, do try to quicken your game. Fast hockey is the order of the day. If you are slow, opposing defenders will give you no chance. If you are faster than they are, you will make ground before they are able to beat you, and be sure you practise hitting that ball—hard and true—along the carpet.

[*Topical Press.*

A PRACTICE GAME.

A Fence and Trees.

HOW TO MAKE SCENERY
FOR MODEL RAILWAYS

REALISM can be given to the model railway if some scenery is added. I have made quite a lot of this and have always used all manner of odd scraps and pieces.

First of all we will start off with some simple hedges and fences. In making these do not try to make them even and solid looking. Get all your edges rugged and your fence bars irregular and different. Plan these sections up in lengths of about 9 inches and make the main parts from 2 inches to $2\frac{1}{2}$ inches high and the tree sets take up to 4 inches in height. I have made quite a few of these sets from the strong lids drapers use on large mantle boxes. Once you have cut up the strips, roughly draw in the fence and an outline for the trees. Don't cut in between the bars, you will only split the cardboard and cause the narrow parts to split. Try to pick out your fence in white with heavy black lines on the underside of bars and on all right-hand sides of posts. Broken irregular stripes on the bars will give the correct impression. You will find small tubes of poster colour paint admirable for this work and it can be used on rough cardboard. For the tree groups get two or three of those twopenny tins of enamel which are sold by handicraft shops. Get two colours of green and some yellow. Cut down a small brush so that you can apply the enamel in daubs and then mix the shades up on the groups. Carefully study any painting or drawing ; posters will give a good idea of the arrangement of these colours. Last of all mark in the tree branches with dark brown and stroke on one with your black enamel. Do not attempt fine detail—strive for bold outline.

Useful small archways are handy and can be made from any box-lid such as one finds on shoe-boxes. If you leave on the side

Trees a Barn and Fence.

strips for strength, you can cut out the opening for your train to pass through. Do not cover with brickpapers at all. Mix up some thin glue and then crush up some old building bricks if you can get them and sprinkle on the glue. Mix up the brick shades and use also some silver sand or plaster powder. The more you mix the shades the better the result. This type of bridge can be used for the end of a line, but a double section could be used to make a complete two-sided bridge. Two similar sections might be used, somewhat apart, to make up a tunnel.

Advertisement hoardings may always be used to fill up gaps in the scenery. These are best made up by getting some strong box lids with fairly stout flaps to keep them in shape. Rigid supports can be fitted to the back of the lid, and the sides of smaller boxes which may carry pictorial advertisements can be glued on, leaving a space between of, say, 2 inches. Make these sets up in threes and then cover the surrounding space with gummed black paper. The border will throw up the coloured picture and cover the cardboard.

Strong box lids which will stand up to a height of about 10 inches can be used to make up the larger groups. One of these

An archway made from the lid of a box.

groups can be seen in the illustration. With a little imagination the clever worker will be able to elaborate these ideas. There is no reason why farmhouses cannot be worked into these set-pieces.

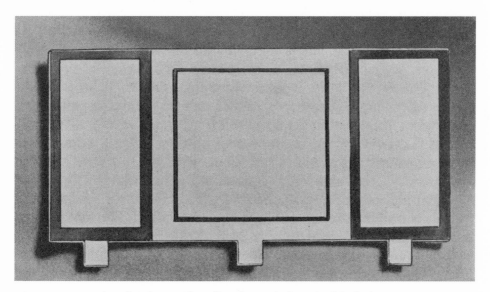

An advertisement hoarding also made from the lid of a box.

An archway and railway cutting.

Do not make all your sets to face the same way, you must reverse some of them. The fence of the farmyard is made in the same way as in the first set and also the trees are treated similarly. Being taller you must fit in the simple bits of strut behind them to save the cardboard from curling under the paint. The old barn roof should be picked out in bright reds and browns and the upright supports in fawn or nigger. Black streaks down the roof will give old-world appearance.

Railway cuttings can be made up very quickly with the aid of long strips of cardboard which can be folded to make the archway or bridge in one end. Make your sides of the cutting about 8 inches high and each side 9 inches long with about 6 inches at the end for the archway. If you can make the sides longer, then do so to suit your own plans. Do not strip off the edge of the lid as this will serve to keep it from bending. Offset the top of the cutting by giving a rugged edge which can be painted in with some dull greens to give the impression of moss and grass. This will outline the paler shade of the actual cutting below. I have used thick distemper, glue and silver sand, glue and broken brick or powdered plaster and even cement on glue. All of these are practical and certainly very effective. The bricks can be indicated by rough broken strokes of black or green paint. Do not attempt to paint complete bricks, only paint odd sides to them.

No railway can be complete without some warehouses. Box-lids can again make up the bulk of these if you plan them carefully. To avoid much tedious cutting out, I suggest that you make the windows on strips of odd cardboard and then glue them on in their proper positions. By this means one can make up whole sets of warehouse scenery in the flat stage and fit it together according to the scene to be made. As shown in the illustration, some small lids can be stood up endways, others, of the larger type can be put lengthways, thereby giving the impression of the storage parts of the warehouse which mostly jut out and give relief to the model. If you used two complete boxes for the ends, the centre section would then stand quite well without further support. To make these sections more useful, I suggest that they are covered with slate-grey paper. The whole surface can be covered.

Strips of the very small red brick paper or the yellow brick paper obtainable from most " Hobbies " shops should now be cut up in widths of about 1 inch. To keep the sections uniform, I suggest that these strips are added at heights of say 4 inches, 8 inches, and a wider strip at the top nearest the roof. Should the warehouse be less than 12 inches in height, then the heights of the strips can be reduced to 3 inches, 6 inches and 9 inches. By working in this way you can add many new pieces in your leisure time and then fit these sections together when making up the full model. This arrangement will allow all sections to be used in any position without looking disjointed. Many variations can be made, such as some pieces being covered with glue and sand, or perhaps with glue and red brick.

Warehouse buildings made from boxes.

[*Fox Photos.*

A model of the *Coronation Scot* in model scenery that is typically British in character.

The windows can be planned on the white cardboard found inside some of the smaller boxes. Draw the windows in lightly first, then fill in the bars with a heavy black crayon. Note the tiny panes of glass and also the few that have got no glass and show quite black. If you line the small windows crossways with a dark blue crayon the effect will be complete. By planning these windows on one long strip you can work much faster and more neatly than if working on single windows. Remember to draw the outer frames in good heavy stokes to give definite outline.

Factory Windows.

68

SOME MORE PARTY GAMES

FOLLOW THE DOTS

ASK each player to put on a small sheet of paper six large dots, in any position. Collect the papers, shuffle them, and hand them again to the players, who have to make a drawing, using the dots as the main framework.

WHO'S WHO

For this game prepare a list of well-known men and women, alive or dead. Dictate their *surnames* to the players, who are required to supply the Christian names. Two points can be given for a name, and one for an initial only, etc. This will be found an excellent test of observation and memory, if the names are carefully selected. They should not, of course, be too generally known.

ON HOLIDAY

Cut out the pictures of well-known resorts from some illustrated holiday guides, eliminate the names, number them, and let competitors make a list of their guesses.

The counties can be written on the pictures if it is desired to make the contest less difficult.

DO YOU KNOW?

Paste on postcards photographs of well-known people that have been cut from newspapers, and number them. Competitors make a list of their guesess.

The competition can be made more difficult by getting the better-known people in unusual surroundings and attitudes.

" SMELLS "

Suspend small quantities of odorous materials in little muslin bags on a string across the room. Fix a numbered label on each. Competitors have to smell the bags without touching them, and record their guesses as to the contents.

SOME MORE PARTY GAMES

POSTMEN

Place in any available spots—round the room, up the stairs—a number of boot boxes, each with a big slit in the lid. In large letters on the lid, write the name of a County.

Prepare a number of small slips, about six times as many as there are players, each bearing the name of a Town. There can be several of each town. Place these slips in a box which remains at a spot which can be called the " Sorting Office."

The game proceeds like this. A player goes to the Sorting Office, takes a slip, puts his name on it, and then finds the appropriate box and " posts " the slip. He then returns for another slip and again seeks the appropriate county box.

Players may not take away more than one slip at a time. When all the slips have been used up, the game finishes, and someone is given the task of collecting the slips, seeing that they have been posted in the right boxes, and counting to ascertain which player posted the greatest number.

NURSERY RHYMES

Hand to competitors postcards (numbered) and announce that each one is to draw something that will represent a well-known Nursery Rhyme. There are dozens of rhymes from which to choose, and you will get some amusing results. Allow five minutes, and place the drawings round the room. Players are then given papers on which to record their guesses, a prize being offered for the most successful. A prize can also be given for the best drawing.

ANIMAL NOISES

The name of an animal is whispered to each of the players. At a given signal the players mingle with one another, all making the noises of the animals they represent. When the signal is given to stop, the players are handed papers and have to write down the names of the animals they have heard—as many as they can remember.

IS YOUR MEMORY GOOD?

There are 34 subjects illustrated on this page. Take a good look at them and memorise them. Close the book and see how many you can remember. A complete list is given on page 76.

AN ATTRACTIVE SHEET OF NON-CURRENT STAMPS.

Non-current : Fifteen Correos, Spain (King Alfonso) ; One Shilling, South Australia (Victoria) ; Five Lei, Roumania ; Three Pies, India (Victoria Jubilee) ; Five Cents, U.S.A. (Columbus Set) ; Six Penny, New South Wales (Victoria) ; Three Cents, U.S.A.

COLLECTING POSTAGE STAMPS

THERE is endless pleasure to be derived from collecting postage stamps and, if you set to work in the proper way, you will find that as the number of your stamps grows more and more, so will the delight of collecting them become greater.

Probably, the first few stamps that attracted your attention were given to you by a friend, or perhaps you took them from a letter that the postman brought to your house. Of course, these are both good ways for helping on your collection, but they are somewhat slow and, in your enthusiasm, you will cast around for quicker methods of adding to the number of your stamps. One excellent plan, at the outset, is to wait until you have saved a little pocket-money and then to buy a packet containing a given number of different stamps. There are packets at all prices ; for 250 different stamps you will probably have to pay about a shilling and for 500 about three shillings. Having made a start, you will find stamps offered for sale in innumerable quarters, from single stamps and penny packets upwards. Later on, you will find that approval sheets will help you to secure some useful bargains. You will be able to read about them in the advertisement columns of your favourite weekly or monthly magazine. Almost as soon as you begin to gather in your stamps you will find that, in some cases, you have two or more alike. The duplicates will prove useful for exchanging with your friends. In these different ways the collection grows and it is marvellous how quickly it grows.

COLLECTING POSTAGE STAMPS

If you want to be proud of your collection and hope that in course of time it may be valuable, never put any torn, dirty or damaged stamps in it. Philatelists are very careful about their stamps and soiled or mutilated copies possess very little attraction for them. Even if it is only a small corner that has been torn off or if two or three of the perforations have disappeared, the stamp has lost most of its interest. Other stamps you should avoid are those that have been heavily postmarked or that have been used for receipts and have been cancelled by means of writing. In addition, you should not be too eager to accept those that have been cut from postcards, embossed envelopes and wrappers.

One penny Red Mauritius, catalogued (unused) at £5,000; (used) at £3,500. The Twopenny Blue is also catalogued at the same values.

One of the first things you will need on settling down to be a philatelist is an album ; but do not buy a splendid album with a leather binding and gilt edges. What spare money you have, spend rather on the stamps and let the album be a cheap one.

But whatever the kind of album, let the arrangement of its contents reveal a tidy and orderly appearance.

Before the stamps are stuck into the album, it is advisable to take the paper off the backs, if somebody else has not done this already. Do not drop the stamps into water, because many of them are printed with inks that will run should the water come in contact with their faces. The proper method is to arrange a number of them, backs up, on a sheet of clean blotting paper and, then, to paint the backs with warm water, using a small brush for the purpose. Perhaps you will have to go over each stamp two or three times with the water ; but very soon the gum will soften and you will be able to peel the paper away. Then, press the stamps between dry blotting paper and they will be ready for the next step.

The next step consists in sorting the stamps into their countries. That done, you take each country and arrange the stamps in the order of their age—the oldest ones first and the recent ones last ; then you place all those of the same age in rows according to their face values, beginning with the low values and ascending to the highest prices. Of course, it is not always an easy matter to tell the age and other particulars of a stamp by looking at it. The post-mark may help, but if it is unused you have not even that shred of evidence. The proper plan is to consult a stamp catalogue and, if you do not possess one, it is often possible to borrow a copy from a friend or the local library. Cheap copies of previous years' editions are frequently offered at half-price and one of these is all that a beginner needs for some years to come.

Five Heller,
Austria.

When you have your stamps correctly arranged, the time has come to stick them into the album. It is advisable to do this very carefully and to try to make each page a picture. The bright colours and the splendid designs will help considerably. What you should aim at is to get the rows straight and to refrain from crowding the stamps together.

For sticking the stamps into the album, it is best to use the hinges specially sold for the purpose. They cost about 6d. per 1,000. Each consists of a thin strip of paper that is gummed on one side.

Three Cents, Canada —
Queen Victoria Jubilee.

First, you fold the strip across the middle, gummed surface outwards ; then you moisten one of the flaps and press it against the back of the stamp and follow this by moistening the other flap and sticking it in the correct position on the page of the album. It may be exacting work, but it is wonderfully fascinating and something in which you can take a real pride.

If you are intent on making your collection something more than a mere assembly of stamps, choose an album consisting of blank pages and devote a certain amount of space to a description of the stamps. At the head of a page, neatly print the name of the country and then, in brackets, give the name of the capital town. In one corner, it will be useful to draw a small sketch map of the country showing its position in the world. All these particulars can be found in your school atlas. Then, above each issue, give its date, and if the stamps show a person's portrait, pencil in the name of the person. Where an animal is depicted, state what it is and, if it is a view, giving the name of the place. By adding all sorts of scraps of information in this way, your album becomes a real live encyclopædia of interesting pictures.

One Guerche,
Abyssinia.

People who do not understand the joys of stamp-collecting look upon stamps as mere scraps of paper with something printed on them. The philatelist, however, has a very different opinion. He knows that his album contains, possibly, hundreds of works of art, and, if he cares to view his treasures through a reading glass, he has what is actually a fine picture gallery. By turning over the pages of his album, he may see the sights of the universe, he can gaze upon the portraits of the world's most noted men and women, he may study a very representative assembly of beasts and birds coming from both sides of the equator and he can learn about history, geography, heraldry, currency and a dozen other subjects. The knowledge that comes from collecting is thus considerable, and there is always the possibility and joy of a valuable rare stamp turning up in some un-looked-for quarter. The approximate values of the various stamps are indicated in the catalogue.

Fifty Haleru, Czechoslovakia ; One Thousand Marks and Five Million (Post-war inflation), Germany ; Twenty Stotinka, Bulgaria ; Ten Cents, France ; Half Mila de Peso, Puerto Rico, and Five Cents, Netherlands.

MEMORY TEST

List of subjects contained in the Test on page 71.

1. Crab	13. Football	24. Stag
2. Fountain Pen	14. Bag	25. Shoe
3. Picture Clip	15. Revolver	26. Scissors
4. Mallet	16. Knife	27. Bus
5. Bearskin	17. Basket	28. Crown
6. Earphones	18. Aeroplane	29. Magnet
7. Plane	19. Signal	30. Wheelbarrow
8. Steps	20. Tweezers	31. Hat
9. Tennis Racket	21. Ship	32. Caterpillar
10. Yacht	22. Fish	33. Iron
11. Pair of Compasses	23. Grandfather Clock	34. Key
12. Engine		

FAR FROM THE MADDING CROWD.

THE CALL OF THE OPEN AIR

THERE is—particularly in these days of machinery and enforced living in towns and cities—a real thrill in being out in the Open Air, away from the madding crowd, following in the tracks of the backwoodsman and the pioneer. . . .

More and more people are taking up pursuits which bring them into the Great Outdoors, and they get to know the thrill of being awake in camp at dawn to hear the morning chorus of the birds, of watching birds and animals at work and play, and photographing a wild animal in natural surroundings, or perhaps of making a hut from branches of trees and dried grass or bracken, and sleeping in it as did the old pioneers. . . .

Summer or winter, there is almost no end to the fascinating activities which are included in what the Boy Scouts know as Outdoor Scouting—the practice of Woodcraft, pioneering, stalking, tracking, exploration and pathfinding—and, of course, camping and hiking.

Woodcraft is really, as the name implies, the craft of living in the woods, which demands a thorough knowledge of backwoodsmanship and nature lore, and how to make the most of natural resources for your own use and comfort—for in camp you should be *comfortable :* only a tenderfoot, or novice, " roughs it " !

You should know how to light a fire and cook your own food, how to look after yourself when without the amenities of civilisation, how to find your way across unknown country.

This last you can do by practice with a map and compass ; by noting the position of the sun by day or the stars by night, or the wind direction if the sun is not visible ; by taking note of landmarks so that if necessary you can find your way back over the route you are following.   This applies just as much to a town as to the country.

If you are without a compass, you can find your direction by

Finding the South with a watch.

the sun in day time (remembering that in England the sun is South at noon, east early in the morning, and west in the evening), and by the moon and stars at night. This will be explained later in an article " Adventures after Dark."

If you have a watch, you can find the South at any time of the day by holding the watch flat, face upwards, so that the hour hand points to the sun. Then lay a pencil across the face of the watch, so that it makes a line from the centre of the dial, and pointing half-way between the figure 12 and the hour hand. This pencil will now point South, the shadow of the match in our design falls straight along the hour hand. (Don't forget, of course, to take into account the hour's variation from sun time on your watch during the summer months.)

The above method works only in the northern hemisphere. South of the equator the *figure* 12 should be turned towards the sun—and the north-south direction line will lie, as before, between the " 12 " and the hour hand.

It is fun to take a map and a compass, and go out exploring, either on foot or awheel, with no fixed route in mind perhaps, but *with some fixed object* other than to cover the greatest number of miles in the shortest possible time.

Ideas such as following old roads or tracks like the Pilgrims' Way, following a river to its source, etc., will suggest themselves, and you can choose any subject for the aim of your exploring trip, according to what are your particular interests. Architecture, photography, tracking, nature study, trees, castles, map-making, scenes of historic events—these are a few suggestions, but whatever your fancy, you can hike or cycle away in search of new ideas on your chosen hobby.

Weather forecasting is an interesting study . . . the old pioneers had no radio to warn them of a gale or a rain belt;

Lenticular, or lens-shaped clouds, indicating warm and squally weather.

but they had their weather signs, just as has many a countryman to-day —and he is more often than not correct !

You will know the old tag, " Red sky at night, shepherd's delight : Red in morning, shepherd's warning "—but do you know that with a yellow sunset there is a chance of wind ; while a pale yellow indicates a likelihood of wet weather. Dew and mist in the early morning augur well for a fine day to come.

The clouds, too, can tell us quite a lot about the weather. " Soft " clouds mean fine weather ; hard-edged clouds—wind.

Lenticular or lens - shaped clouds, like those shown in our first cloud illustration, indicate warm

Thread-like wisps of white cirrus clouds or " Mares' Tails," indicating a depression.

and squally weather. Thread-like wisps of white cirrus clouds (Mares' Tails) indicate a depression. High cumulus (Alto-cumulus) clouds indicate disturbed conditions in the intermediate levels of the atmosphere ; and when cumulus clouds increase rapidly in bulk and height, they usually foretell a coming thunderstorm.

These are only a few of the interesting activities which are opened up to those who answer the call of the Open Air. Some other suggestions are made and dealt with in more detail in later articles.

Let us get out on the trail, let us follow in the footsteps of the explorers, let us capture the spirit of the Outdoors. . . .

Alto-cumulus or high cumulus clouds, indicating disturbed conditions in the intermediate levels of the atmosphere.

Cumulus clouds. When these increase rapidly in bulk and height, they usually portend a coming thunderstorm.

"WELL HIT, SIR!"

[*Fox Photos.*

BE A BETTER CRICKETER

LIKE every other boy, you want to be a good cricketer; but you will never be much more than mediocre unless you set out to do one particular job in cricket really well. For example, if you are keen on batting, practise wielding the willow for all you are worth; similarly, if you favour bowling or wicket-keeping, let these receive especial attention. On the other hand, good all-rounders *are* made as well as born, and if you manage to take wickets and keep your end up with the bat, there is no reason why you should not try to become this asset to every side—the man who can turn his hand to anything in an emergency.

FIELDING

Let us take fielding first, for it is important that *every* player should be useful in this direction. It is of no use being a weak link —the player who continually fumbles catches or who cannot be relied upon to stop a good, fast one when placed at mid-on.

Learn to catch at every possible opportunity. Sling the ball up and catch it. Get other players to throw the ball to you—as hard as they like. Good catching means wickets just as well as good bowling.

How far can you throw a ball? This is a very important matter to the young fielder, for he may be put " out in the country," and be expected not only to stop boundaries, but to throw in quickly and well. Therefore practise pitching in hard. Many players " in the country " are so poor at throwing that someone else has to be stationed between them and the wicket-keeper for every ball they take.

Backing-up is very important in fielding, too. In other words, it is the duty of every player to anticipate what might happen as a result of a bad throw to the wicket-keeper or bowler. The ball may come in too fast, be missed, and give the batsmen a chance of an extra run or so on the overthrow. A player who backs up can take that ball and return it to its proper place so swiftly that, if the batsmen *do* try to steal a run, one of them may be run out.

There are fielders who never seem able to take a ball on the run. They must stop it with their feet before picking it up. Watch a County player race up alongside the ball and, in an instant, turn and send the ball streaking back to the wicket-keeper. And the ball is kept low, too. No skying so that time is wasted.

If your fielding position is close in, there is some good practice to be gained from trying to hit the wickets. How pleased you feel with yourself when a smart throw-in hits the wicket and almost runs out the batsman. Perhaps you actually do get his wicket ! A good eye and a strong right arm are what you need to become this valuable fielder.

One last point about fielding. Do you stand exactly where the bowler or your captain has placed you, or do you draw in gradually ? The correct thing to do is to move to a spot where your cricketing second sense sends you. Often by coming in a few paces you are able to make a smart catch which would not have been possible from your original position. On the other hand, it is not wise to wander.

BATTING

The young batsman who aspires to play in good-class cricket should spend as much time as possible watching the best players he can find. Make friends with your County players. Obtain the

BE A BETTER CRICKETER

assistance and advice of the best club men you know. They will be only too happy to help you. Watch the best County batsmen make their strokes. Watch the bowlers take the wickets. Then go and watch *mediocre* cricket. Immediately you will notice the colossal difference, and it is when you realise what is good and what is bad cricket that you are gaining knowledge to help you in your cricketing future.

[*Topical Press.*

TIPS FROM THE COACH.

Most young batsmen have the ambition to become a second Jack Hobbs or Don Bradman; but you will never become first-class if you adopt a cramped, awkward stance at the wicket. Admitted, there *are* first-class players who do little according to the accepted theories of batsmanship, but in the main the best and most consistent players are those whose batting is played according to " the book."

It is important that you keep a straight bat, with the right leg firm and the left shoulder well forward. You must never be afraid of any type of bowling, even the fastest. A good plan practised by many promising players is to hammer a big staple into the ground and place the right foot in it. The idea is that this foot shall always remain firm no matter how difficult the bowling may be. So often a player gets, for example, a crack on the knee, and then for ever afterwards automatically moves away from the ball when it is straight, leaving the wicket unprotected. Never be scared of any ball !

[*Sport & General.*

How to hold the bat.

How should you hold your bat ? Here is the advice of the great Dr. Grace. He said : "From my own experience I have always found it to my advantage to hold the bat half-way up the handle, and this happy medium I recommend for adoption, as thereby you can control it as effectively as if held nearer to the blade, and the benefits incidental to the extra length are very important. To hold it higher in the handle neutralises this advantage, as the bat is not so well or so firmly grasped, and the power of hitting at a ball with certainty is considerably lessened."

It is waste of energy, and often fatal, to lunge at every ball. This is exactly what the bowler wants you to do. On the other hand, do not be caught in two minds. Always have a clear-cut idea of what you intend to do with the ball coming down. You might adopt as your motto, " If in doubt, play it out ! " In other words, when in doubt play the stroke out without attempting to hit.

Beware of playing forward. Notice how a bowler will sometimes run half-way down the pitch as he bowls the ball, expecting a simple return catch. Do not "peck" at the ball. This will cause the field to draw in and you may send up the easiest of catches.

The business of run-making itself is full of difficulties. How often has a wicket been lost through hesitancy on the part of one of the batsmen. *Don't* hesitate. If your partner calls, back him up by running. Don't run half-way, yell " No ! " and rush back for all you are worth.

Notice in big matches how sometimes the simplest snick makes a run. The ball rolls along the pitch and the batsmen take a run " with the ball," so to speak. It looks so neat and it usually draws applause from the spectators, who appreciate such excellent understanding between the batsmen.

How to hold the ball.   [*Fox Photos.*

In connection with the making of every possible run, nothing worries a bowler more than to see these singles being made, which so quickly spoil his average. He gets annoyed, and the near-fielders begin to grow uncomfortable.

How do you run between the wickets—in what position do you hold your bat ? There is only one position ! Hold your bat in front of you, diagonally. The reason should be fairly obvious, although so few young cricketers realise the value of running in

85

A missed catch sometimes makes all the difference between victory and defeat.

this way.   The bat is well in front of the player and in the right position should a smart throw to the wicket cause the batsman to race to the crease.   Also, holding the bat thus allows the players to run without a clumsy action.   Try the movement and see how it improves *your* running between the wickets.

What sort of batsman are you when once you arrive at the wicket ?   So often, despite every word of advice from captain or vice, despite warnings from those who have already been in to bat, a youngster goes out to " Have a slosh ! "   Such a player is not working for his side, but for himself.   And when the bowling and fielding are keen he is soon trapped and bowled or caught.   Then comes the terrible moment of walking back to the pavilion, knowing he has let his side down, and realising that the other players know it, too ! There is no excuse for the " Have a slosh-er " ! You should take as your slogan the words of a famous County captain : " Take care of your stumps and the runs will take care of themselves ! "

BOWLING

Many young players have ruined any chance of becoming brilliant bowlers by their methods of practice. They will bowl and bowl until they are absolutely played out, and this will go on day after day. Never bowl after your freshness has departed.

It is not wise to mix styles of bowling. Adopt one and stick to it. It is impossible to be a fast, medium and slow bowler all in one.

When taking part in a match, watch the other bowlers before you—and watch how the batsmen play the bowling. Every batsman has a weak spot in his armour somewhere, and if you can find it before your turn comes, you may quite easily bring about the downfall of a troublesome partnership.

Patience and perseverence are of paramount importance to the bowler. Keep pegging away. There is no reason why you should always bowl for the middle stump. Try the off, try the leg side, try a ball away from the wicket. Do not panic if you are being hit. There are some days when the pitch is unkind to every type of bowler.

THE WICKET-KEEPER

The golden rule for young wicket-keepers is to take a stance as near the wicket as possible. This will save the stealing of runs, and will give you an opportunity of stumping. The farther you are from the batsman the more will he be inclined to take liberties. Let the ball come to you and you will save many a painful finger.

With some bowling, of course, you *must* stand well back—this is unavoidable. But it is often possible for the wicket-keeper and bowler to have a pre-arranged plan whereby, suddenly, the wicket-keeper comes in—and brings off a nice piece of stumping through the batsman thinking he was some distance away !

MEMORY AND SPEED TEST.

The following articles are numbered 1 to 5. Observe these articles and their numbers carefully and then see how many seconds it takes you to fill in on the thirty tabulated drawings below, the correct numbers for every article.

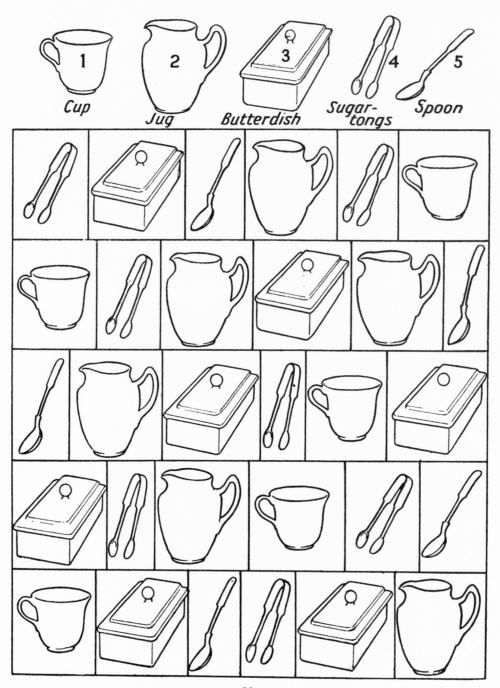

THE BLIND-WORM OR SLOW-WORM. *[M. H. Crawford.*
Such remnants of limbs as it possesses are hidden beneath its skin. In spite of its name, it has, as will be seen in the picture, bright but small eyes.

OUT-OF-DOORS. II

WHAT TO LOOK FOR IN SUMMER

THE warmer days of June, July and August cause a slowing down of bird song. They are now too busy feeding young to sing much, and the nightingale whose song delighted those who live in the south, can now only croak !

The badly-named blind-worm or slow-worm may now be seen sunning itself on a bank or in a woodland glade. It is neither blind, nor slow, and is not a worm ! It is not even a snake, but a legless lizard, and perfectly harmless. Growing to just over a foot long, it has a metallic-looking back and olive-brown sides.

The grass snake, too, is about in the woods, but is also quite harmless, indeed useful, as it eats slugs, worms and other ground pests. It may grow to a length of nearly four feet, has dark markings on the *sides* but none on the back, and a yellow collar below the head, which gives it the name of ring snake. The soft, white eggs will be found in farmyard manure heaps. Our only dangerous reptile is the adder, or viper, which loves hot, sunny banks and open spaces. But it will seldom attack anyone unless cornered, and as a rule will quickly slither away when disturbed. The " V " mark on the head, zig-zag line down the back, and thick body will distinguish it, and it seldom grows more than two feet long. Tales of "poisonous snakes" over four feet long that you read about at this time of year are just nonsense.

Very interesting caterpillars can be found on certain trees during summer, and it is a fascinating pastime to keep them in boxes with fresh food-plants, and watch their development into the chrysalis stage. The hawk moth caterpillars will be found on various trees,

The grass snake.

and if we find one of the death's head moth in a potato field, we shall indeed be lucky, for this is a real prize and a rarity. This strange caterpillar squeaks when touched, but is incapable of harm. The "woolly bear" caterpillar which hurries across our path is that of the garden tiger moth, and only the cuckoo will eat this hairy creature.

In the woods the noisy, harsh note of the jay warns other birds of the fact that we are approaching. You must get a glimpse of this rather pretty member of the crow family, for its head and wings are most beautifully marked with bright blue and black. Another inhabitant of the woods will be heard "drumming" on the tall trees. If we keep still the drummer will come into view, searching spirally up the trunk for insects. It is the great spotted woodpecker, black and white with a red head. The green woodpecker is larger, has a fondness for orchards, and is handsomely coloured with green and yellow, and also has a red head. Its favourite food consists of ants, and we may often see it searching an ant-hill and with its enormously long tongue licking up ants and their larvæ.

The viper or adder.

When you are out on the moors or heather-covered common, keep a watch for the red grouse, for it is not only in Scotland that this bird breeds, and a hasty whirr of wings from under your feet will often betray the whereabouts of a brood of young.

There is another interesting creature among the heather—the potter wasp, which makes a nest of sand cemented together by the insect. In this it lays

An otter chasing a salmon.

The Red Grouse.

eggs, and proceeds to gather small caterpillars, which it stings into a stupor, placing them in the nest as fresh food for the wasp-grubs which will hatch !

A quiet hour near the river bank in the evening may be spent listening for the whistle of the otter, an animal that loves the water. Parents will be bringing their cubs down for a swimming lesson, and if you see a smooth, well-worn slope down into the river, you may be sure you have seen the otter's slide, which it enjoys as much as any schoolboy !

The otter is a great fisherman, and woe betide the unsuspecting salmon or trout that comes within view. Although perfectly at home in the water, swimming by means of sinuous twists of its long body and tail, or by strokes of its feet, the otter is tolerably active on land, often covering quite long distances between streams. Its " holt," as the den is called, is either a burrow, a rock crevice or a hollow beneath a tree root, usually near the water, and in this, on a bed of rushes, the young are born.

The badger is a much commoner animal than is generally supposed, and should you find short, black-and-white hairs near

The Green Woodpecker.
Notice how it supports itself on its stiff, strong tail.

Great Spotted Woodpecker and Nest.

a large hole under a tree-trunk, you have probably discovered its home. But you will not see these interesting creatures unless you stay up until it is dark, and keep absolutely still and silent. Only then will the badgers come out on their nightly prowl. A slight move or noise, and they will flash back to the " set," as the burrow is called, never to venture out again that night.

The cubs, usually two or three in number, are born in spring or summer in a special nursery in the burrow, which the female badger lines with grass or moss.

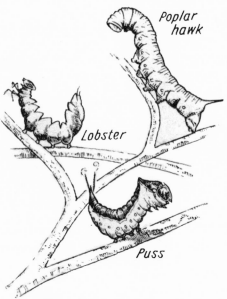

Caterpillars of the Poplar hawk moth, the Lobster moth and the Puss moth.

A Badger.

[Charles Reid.

A MEMORY AND SPEED TEST

The following animals' heads are numbered 1 to 5. Observe these numbers carefully and then see how many seconds it takes you to fill in on the twenty-five tabulated drawings below, the correct number for every animal's head.

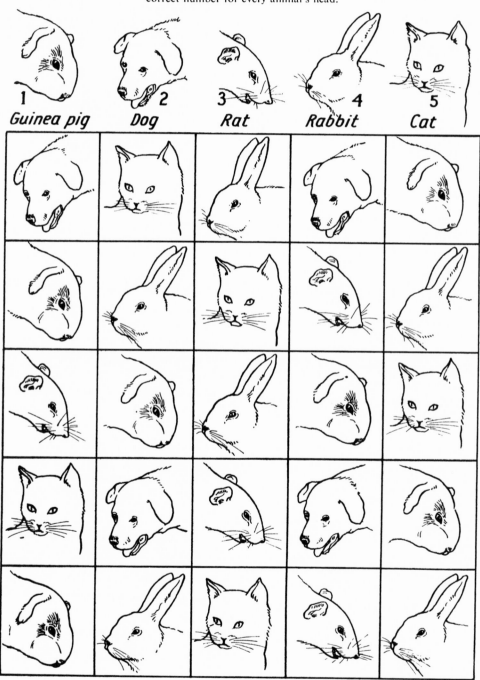

1	2	3	4	5
Guinea pig	Dog	Rat	Rabbit	Cat

THE ANIMATED MATCHES.

SOME TRICKS WITH MATCHES

MUCH fun can be had from the following very simple tricks, for which practically the only accessory needed is a box of ordinary wooden matches. Simplicity is the keynote of these tricks, but they are none the less puzzling and amusing.

Animated Matches.—After having broken off the heads of a few matches, lay the wooden sticks like the spokes of a wheel on the surface of some water in a saucer, with a space about an inch in diameter in the centre. The water must be quite still. Roll a slip of blotting paper about three inches by twelve inches loosely into a tube about as large round as a sixpence, and then let the end just touch the surface of the water in the centre of the saucer; a minute current is raised, and the pieces of match are drawn towards the blotting paper. To make the matches move away from the centre, instead of the blotting paper use a small piece of soap cut to the shape of a tube or cylinder. When it touches the water, the matches immediately scatter in all directions.

How to Change Four Squares to Three.—Place twelve matches to form four equal squares as in the first illustration, and then remove and replace four matches so as to make only three squares of the same size as the others. It is accomplished in the manner depicted in the second and third diagrams.

A Match that Walks.—This trick is accomplished by bending a match in half, *i.e.* making a prong, and on the top of the prong pasting or fixing a vignetted picture of a man. Next place the inside of the prong upon the edge of the blade of a knife, and hold the latter parallel with the table, so that both ends of the match just touch it. The match will then "walk" from one end of the knife to the other, without any effort of your own. This can also be done with two matches joined at the ends by splitting one and sharpening the other. They may also be bent in the centre to impart a knee-like appearance.

The Square of Nine.—Form a square of eight piles, each containing three matches, so that each side of the square contains nine ; there should be twenty-four matches in all. Add one, then three, and afterwards four matches in such a way that in each case there are still only nine matches in each side and at top and bottom.

The problem is solved in the following manner :—

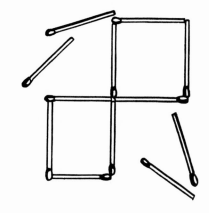

FIG. 1.

```
III      III      III
III               III
III      III      III
```

Remove a match from the top left-hand corner, and add it to the three in the centre of the top row, now add an extra match to the three in the centre of the left-hand row.

FIG. 2.

```
 II     IIII     III
IIII             III
III      III     III
```

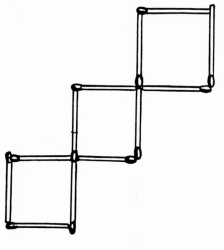

How to change four squares into three.

Next take one match from the top right-hand corner and add it to the pile in the centre of the top row, take one from the left-hand bottom corner, and add it to the pile just above it, and one from the right-hand bottom corner to the pile above that also.   Add three extra matches to make each centre pile consist of five, and each corner two.

FIG. 3.

II	IIIII	II
IIIII		IIIII
II	IIIII	II

Take one match from each corner and add it to each of the centre piles.   Then add an extra match to each of the centre piles.

FIG. 4.

I	IIIIIII	I
IIIIIII		IIIIIII
I	IIIIIII	I

In each case the sides of the square contain nine matches.

How to Multiply a Number of Matches.—To do this, lay the matches to form Roman numerals, *e.g.* three matches will make four or six, *i.e.* IV, VI ; two matches will make five, V ; nine matches will make three dozen, XXXVI.

Another method is to make letters with the matches, and to spell the number, *e.g.* eleven matches will make nine, NINE.

In order to make nine matches into three and a half dozen, make two heaps, one containing three, and the other, six matches, *i.e.* three and a half dozen.

A match that walks.

SKATING FOR BEGINNERS

WHAT is the difference between roller and ice skating ? Not a very great deal, except that roller skating is very much slower. Most of the fascinating figures produced in ice skating can be performed by the expert roller skater, but they take much longer and certainly require a great deal more effort.

Nowadays, ice skating is far more popular than roller skating, and the art of keeping your feet can be acquired fairly quickly if you have confidence. The first essential is balance, with the body thrown well forward. To hold yourself upright invites the fatal backward slip, when the feet slide forward and you find yourself hitting the ice very hard.

You are bound to have falls at the beginning, but do not be disheartened. Above all, avoid the fault of bending the knees, waving the arms, and taking shuffling, untidy movements. If you watch a good skater performing, you will see that he keeps only one foot on the ice at a time, and makes his strokes as long as possible.

A HELPING HAND.   [*Mirrorpic.*

The beginner need not consider strokes beyond three to five yards, but gradually as he gains confidence he will increase his distance.

If both feet should come down on the ice together, *keep them parallel* ! It is only when the feet go off at different angles that the inevitable tumble results.

As you improve, you will find yourself automatically placing more weight on your skates and moving on the *inside edge* of the skates. At all costs, avoid the bad fault of sliding along on the flat of the skates.

ICE HOCKEY

One of the most strenuous of games, Ice Hockey is played at great speed. A disc made of vulcanised rubber and known as a " puck " is played on an ice-rink by two teams, consisting of six players each, equipped with hockey sticks.

Each player has a large number on the back of his sweater, for the purpose of identification.

ICE HOCKEY—A THRILLING MOMENT.

A PAPER LADDER

TAKE a long, narrow strip of paper and roll it up tightly into a cylinder as in Figure 1.

Then tear out, or with scissors or a sharp knife cut out the portion indicated by dotted lines, the portion cut out extending round at least half the circumference of the cylinder. The result

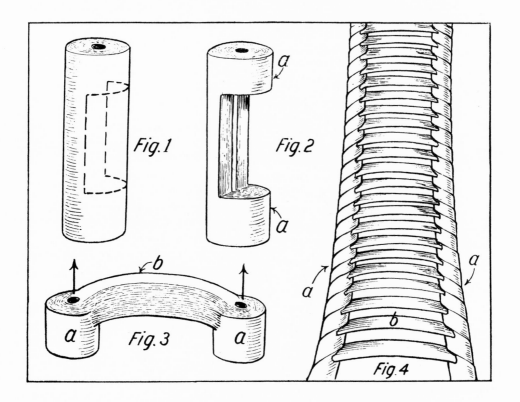

will be Figure 2. Then bend over the two solid end portions *a* at right angles to give Figure 3.

Next, with the thumb and finger, or a fine-nosed pair of pliers, or a pin, raise the centres of the end cylinders *a* in the direction of the arrows and continue pulling on these until the ladder is formed as shown in part in Figure 4, the centre part *b*, bridging the end cylinders *a*, supplying the rungs of the ladder.

ORGANISING A PAPER CHASE

MOST land-owners are kindly folk, but they are not very pleased if those who organise paper-chases consider only their sport and fail to carry out certain unwritten laws.

When organising a paper-chase, therefore, it is well to remember the following points :

1. Impress upon all taking part in the chase that gates must be closed and hedges left undamaged. Fields of crops should be skirted ; never trampled upon.

2. Do not use too much paper. The trail should be clear but not untidy.

3. Choose a starting-place that is not too open. This gives the hares a chance to get out of sight before the hounds set off in pursuit. The time allowed for the former to get away must, of course, depend upon the length of the run, but it should not be less than five minutes or more than a quarter of an hour.

4. The hares must not be very much faster runners than the hounds. Indeed, they should be about equal to the best of the hounds.

5. Avoid towns as much as possible, even though it may be exciting to run through a main street. In any case, the local police may object to the laying of a trail.

6. Do not attempt to hold a paper-chase when there is a very high wind, or the trail will be lost almost at once and the whole affair develop into a game of hide-and-seek.

7. See that everyone is dressed for the occasion. Shorts and singlets or jerseys are best, with rubber-soled shoes for the feet. Spiked shoes are permissible, but are not really necessary in an ordinary paper-chase.

8. When laying false trails, the hares must be honest and see that the main trail is unbroken.

9. Do not make the run so long that the hounds grow weary and drop out before the end. The successful paper-chase is the one in which everyone finishes fairly fresh, with the hares overtaken by the triumphant hounds, or just beating them.

10. Finally, see that the paper used is in small pieces, and impress upon the hares not to have large stocks left at the end of the run. They should scatter the paper so evenly that it just lasts out.

TRACKS OF A DOG (above) AND CAT (below).

WALKING ON A NEWSPAPER

EVERYONE reads a newspaper. The news, articles and pictures tell us a great many interesting things. But every time we go for a walk—particularly in the country, through the woods and over the fields—we are *walking* on a newspaper. It doesn't cost us a penny, and yet, if only we know how to read it, it can give us many hours of fun and interest.

The ground itself is this newspaper—and the ability to read it is known as tracking. Just how exciting tracking can be is shown by the fact that tracks have often been the means of bringing to book a murderer, or of clearing up other mysteries which have baffled detectives who were not expert trackers.

Apart from this, it is great fun to be able to identify from a track who, or what, has passed, and how long ago ; to be able to follow a trail (a series of tracks) ; and such activities can add greatly to the enjoyment of a hike or nature ramble.

Most people could tell at a glance whether an impression in the ground was made by a human being or an animal ; but a good tracker can give the name of the animal—can, by studying a series of the tracks, give the height and many other characteristics of a man—and can distinguish between the tracks of various kinds of birds, telling whether they are birds which spend most of their lives in the water, on the ground, or in trees.

Try it next time you are out hiking. You may not have much success at first, but keep practising . . . and the more you practise the more interested you will become in this fascinating hobby.

Summer or winter—at any time of the year—you can get out on the trail . . . and you will easily realise what a great opportunity a fall of snow provides for tracking.

WALKING ON A NEWSPAPER

Tracking is really a practical " follow-up " to information gained by keen observation . . . It can lead to the detection of a " wanted " man through the observing of his style of walking, his footwear, clothes, a characteristic mark, or a

Tracks of hind paws—cat (left) and dog (right).

distinguishing habit such as the twitching of an eye. It can lead to the tracking down of a stolen or " wanted " car or cycle through the observing of its particular tyre tread (and whether this tyre is old or new), its number plate, colour, design, etc.

Moreover, the tracker will, if he is also a good stalker, find his knowledge and observation a royal road to the discovery and study of animals and birds in their natural ways of life.

If you come across a track, and are interested in following the movements of the man, animal, or vehicle which made it, you must first get a good " picture " of it in your mind, so that you can recognise it when you see it again. If you do not care to trust your memory, you may find it best to make a little drawing of the track.

Then you can follow the trail along, watching out for, and taking note of the particular track as you come across it.

You will find it difficult, especially when working on a road or on smooth ground, to distinguish tracks if you look from directly overhead. In this case try getting your eye on ground level, and looking *along* the ground, towards the sun. You can then often pick out a track quite clearly.

Another tip to help you guard against losing sight of the trail is to keep the distance between each track in mind. If one should then be obscured, you may be able to locate it by knowing roughly

Tracks of front paws—cat (left) and dog (right).

where it *ought* to be in relation to the preceding one—that is assuming whatever you are trailing has proceeded without interruption.

You should also look out for other signs, such as disturbed stones, scratches, or other marks, trampled grass, etc.   This will help you to pick up the trail again.

Should you, however, come to a place where you have lost all trace, leave something to mark the position of the last track, and then " cast about "—that is, search around about twenty or thirty—or more—yards from this centre.   In this way you should eventually locate any continuation of the trail.

*   *   *

Those who study animal and bird tracks often like to take plaster casts, thus providing themselves with permanent records of some of the best examples of tracks which they have recognised.

Plaster of Paris (of which the casts are made) is easily obtainable, and quite cheap, but it must be absolutely fresh, and must be kept in an airtight tin, or it will become stale and not set properly when mixed with water.

Fore and hind feet of Grey Squirrel.

The track of which it is desired to make a cast should first be carefully " cleaned "—that is, any loose grass, twigs, etc. should be removed, *without*, naturally, damaging the track in any way.

Now take a quantity of water in a mug, and add the plaster to it, stirring all the while, until you have a thick, creamy substance which can be poured on to the track. In order to keep the liquid plaster in place should the track be on a slope, a " surround " will be necessary. It can be made of cardboard, or, if you have none with you, of twigs, mud, or other natural materials.   Keep on adding the mixture, so that you obtain a thick cast which will not break.

Fore and hind feet of Red Squirrel.

The cast will not take very long to set, unless you have made the plaster too thin—but the exact time will,

WALKING ON A NEWSPAPER

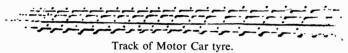

Track of Motor Car tyre.

of course, depend on various conditions of weather, etc. Not until it is perfectly dry should the cast be dug up and cleaned. The addition of the name of the animal and the date the track was " taken " will make your cast an interesting possession.

*   *   *

Some of the greatest fun in tracking can be had in following a trail laid by someone on ahead . . . and you will be able to think up any number of exciting games in connection with this. The

" hunted " man may be (for the occasion) a spy, a criminal fleeing from justice, an escaped convict, or what you will.

Tracks of hedgehog (left) ; stoat (centre) ; and rabbit (right).

You will find that keen observation will keep you on the trail, and you will find how necessary it is not only to be able to pick up footprints, but to notice other signs, such as scratches on trees, newly-turned stones, hairs or pieces of torn clothing on bushes, fences or gates.

Where a trail is being deliberately laid by someone for the benefit of those following, it will—and often must—be laid without artificial means such as chalk or paper. In this case you must be on the look-out for *alterations to nature*, such as a broken twig, a beech leaf placed on an oak tree, etc. This is known as a nature trail, and calls for a keen eye in the following. There are unlimited fields of exploration in this subject of tracking, and once you make a start, you will find your interest growing day by day. You will want to continue with your hobby until you have thoroughly mastered it, and can read the ground just as easily as you can read an ordinary newspaper.

Tracks of moorhen (left) ; pheasant (centre) ; and wild duck (right).

WOODCOCK FEEDING.

TRACKS ARE ALWAYS EASIER TO FOLLOW IN THE SNOW.

THE HORSESHOE PUZZLE

HAVING cut out a paper horseshoe and marked the nail holes as shown in Figure 1, the problem is with only two cuts of a pair of scissors, to cut the horseshoe into seven parts, each part containing one nail hole.

Figure 2 shows how this can be done.

First, the cut *a-b* is made, severing the paper containing nail hole 4.

Then the two parts A and B are placed on top of one another and folded through holes 2 and 6 so that holes, 1 and 3, 5 and 7, come one over the other, and the second cut *c-d* is made as shown in Figure 2, thus cutting the parts A and B into three pieces each, each containing a nail hole as required.

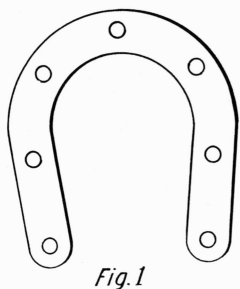

Fig. 1

Although this seems extremely-simple when clearly e x p l a i n e d a n d illustrated, you will f i n d v e r y f e w people able to solve the puzzle for them-selves when con-fronted with the plain horseshoe as illustrated in Figure 1, and told to cut it into seven pieces, each containing one nail hole, with only two cuts of the scissors.

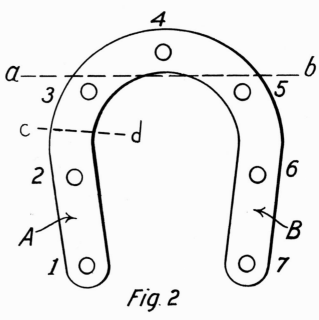

Fig. 2

HOW TO MAKE
A WEATHER-TELLER

W̲E all know that a piece of seaweed, because of the salt in it, will tell us the state of the atmosphere. Hang it on a wall and when rain is coming it will be soft and limp, whilst if it is going to be fine the seaweed will be quite crisp and dry. But we haven't always a piece of seaweed handy, so here is a simple way to make a weather indicator. Dissolve salt water in a cup until no more salt can be dissolved. Cut out from bright pink blotting paper five or six round pieces of varying sizes and shape the edges like petals as shown in our photograph. Twist three pieces of wire together to form a stalk and then fasten the paper rounds one above the other on the wire as shown and bend the end of the wire over to keep the paper petals in place. Soak the blotting-paper in the salt solution. Add a few green leaves to make the flower look more real. When the weather is likely to be fine, your flower will be white (covered with dry white salt crystals), but if the air is damp and rain is coming, the flower will turn a deep pink.

[*S. Leonard Bastin.*

When the weather is likely to be fine, the flower will be white with the dry salt crystals, but if rain is coming it will be a deep pink. The petals are made of bright pink blotting-paper soaked in a strong salt solution.

An interesting weather-telling bird, as shown in our pictures, can be made from a fir cone. Put the cone in a rather warm oven until it is so dry that the scales will open widely. The cone will then be very sensitive to variations in the moisture of the atmosphere.

HOW TO MAKE A WEATHER-TELLER

The cone scales closed for wet weather.

When the air is dry, and the weather is likely to be fine, the scales will be wide open. If the conditions are unsettled the scales will close partly, whilst, when rain is at hand, they will be tightly closed.

The cone forms the body of the bird. The legs are made from wire, each one being formed of three pieces twisted together. Open out the wires at one end to form the feet. The legs can be attached to the cone with sealing-wax or gum and the feet can be stuck on to a little card stand. The neck and head of the bird are cut from stout card and are pushed into a slit made in the end of the cone. Mark in the eyes of the bird with ink.

A very interesting weather-teller, too, may be made with a few flowers of the everlasting type, or such as dandelions. Cut the flowers, as they are on the point of opening, with stalks about two inches long and insert about three parts of an inch of each stalk in a hole in a moist sponge. If the weather continues fine the sponge will dry and the flowers close. When rain is coming the sponge will become moist and the flowers open.

Photos]   [*S. Leonard Bastin.*
A Bird Weather-teller.
Cone scales open for fine weather.

"THOUGHT READING"

IN " Thought Reading " one of the exponents is blindfolded and remains upon the stage while the other moves among the audience, borrowing for a moment, watches, knives, coins, cheques, railway tickets, etc. The latter then asks: "What is this?" and the assistant tells the name of the article, its value (in the case of a coin or cheque), the number or date it bears, etc. The whole feat is worked by an elaborate system of codes. Usually the first letter of a word or sentence is the index.

It may be helpful in the early stages to have a code and use sentences of which only the first letter of each is to be noted, e.g. suppose the name wanted is " Peter Smith." The questioner would say :—

P.	Pay attention	S.	Say what you think.
E.	Everything all right ?	M.	Much faster.
T.	Try hard.	I.	If you please.
E.	Entails much thought ?	T.	Tell me.
R.	Ready ?	H.	Hurry.

This, however, is so obvious that it is advisable to code the letters, e.g.

A	= G	H	= Z	O	= S	V	= L
B	= F	I	= Y	P	= R	W	= K
C	= E	J	= X	Q	= Q	X	= J
D	= D	K	= W	R	= P	Y	= I
E	= C	L	= V	S	= O	Z	= H
F	= B	M	= U	T	= N		
G	= A	N	= T	U	= M		

and then the name given would be coded something like the following :

P	=	R	Ready ?
E	=	C	Concentrate.
T	=	N	Now, think.
E	=	C	Come along now.
R	=	P	Please hurry.
S	=	O	Only two names.
M	=	U	Understand ?
I	=	Y	You ought to know.
T	=	N	Now.
H	=	Z	Zounds varlet, hurry.

As a further example we will assume that the following is the code for numbers :

B	= 0	N	= 5
O	= 1	D	= 6
P	= 2	S	= 7
X	= 3	J	= 8
T	= 4	H	= 9

The number on a railway ticket is, we will say, 2754. The examiner would ask, " Please Say Number for This." That is only a simple illustration given for the purpose of explaining the principle.

A much more complex arrangement would be used in an advanced code, and below are given a few general codes, which, if perfectly committed to memory, and the performer moving amongst the audience possesses the ability readily to construct sentences on given lines, should enable a successful and mystifying performance to be given. It is well to employ the phonetic system entirely, and though to one unacquainted with it, it is apt to be a little puzzling at first, practice soon makes perfect, and it is surprising how it simplifies the questions and prevents them from being made too obvious and long. For example, again assume the code is the first letter of each word, and take the word PENNY (phonetically PENI). The assistant would be asked some such question as : " Please Explain the Nature and Intrinsic worth of this." Often some words that have nothing to do with the code will have to be worked into the sentence in order to make it natural, and one way to avoid misleading the assistant is to drop the voice slightly when saying these words and just as slightly to emphasize the code words, or *vice versa*, or the superfluous words may even be slightly blurred.

Here is another code for numbers :—

1.	Us.	6.	Is or on.
2.	Here or in.	7.	This.
3.	Me or My.	8.	What or That.
4.	Tell or take.	9.	Please.
5.	Now or quick.	0.	Say.

The sentences for single numbers might be something like the following : " Give *us* the number " ; " The number *here* " ;

" Give *me* the number " ; " *Tell* the number " ; " Number, *quick* ? " etc.

Perhaps some combinations in this code might read awkwardly, but a ready wit would soon put that right. For example, 2468, the sentence " Here tell (or take) is (or on) that (or what) " may be made. " Here, tell me the number on that."

To describe articles handed up for examination the following code will be useful :

Tell me.	Halfpenny.	You can tell me	
Tell quickly.	Penny.	this.	Pencil.
Tell us.	Sixpence.	Say this.	Cigar.
Tell.	Shilling.	Say now.	Cigarette.
Now tell.	Two shillings.	Please this.	Pipe.
Tell this.	Half-crown.	Quickly.	Ring.
Here, tell.	Ten shilling note.	Well, this.	Visiting card.
Look here, tell.	Pound note.	This, please.	Purse.
Can you tell		And this.	Handbag.
this ?	Cheque.	And this,	
What this ?	American coin.	please.	Programme.
What now ?	Chinese coin.	Reply this.	Railway ticket.
Guess this.	English coin.	Here, here.	Photograph of a
What here ?	French coin.		lady.
What say ?	Russian coin.	Here ?	Photograph of a
What have I ?	German coin.		gentleman.
What is this ?	Watch.	And here ?	Photograph of a
Now this ?	Knife.		child.
Please say this.	Pocket-book.	Here what ?	Photograph of
Sharp !	Scissors.		scenery.
Call this.	Chain.	Here this ?	Photograph of a
Quickly these.	Keys.		building.

Certain articles may be described at length, and it is well to make a code for describing in detail many common articles, e.g. a watch :

What is this ?	A watch.	Well the maker ?	Waltham.
And it is made		(Using the phonetical alphabetical	
of—?	Gold.	code Wlthm).	
It is a—?	Silver watch.		
Made of—?	Gunmetal.	It has—?	A hunting case.

Use the numerical code for the number of the watch, also for the time.

A sentence in which the first letter of each word spells the value may be added in the code for the valuation of a foreign coin. The date on coins and cheques can be arrived at by the numerical code already given. It is often well to have a signal as to whether it is the numerical or alphabetical code that is being used, and a little cough may serve as an indicator. Sometimes one question allows of two or three others that have been explained by the first. For example, supposing a photograph has been handed up, and the remark was " and here," showing it was the photograph of a child. The blindfolded performer would say : " A photograph " and the other performer would say : " And of what ? " to elicit the reply : " A child."

Clothes are often described, and the principal code needed is in regard to the colour of the articles.

Tell the colour.	White.	What colour ?	Brown.
The colour ?	Yellow.	Say the colour.	Black.
Yes, the colour ?	Grey.	I am touching a	
What is the		—?	A lady.
colour ?	Blue.	Whom am I	
Colour, please ?	Pink.	touching ?	A gentleman.
Now the colour ?	Red.	And here is —?	A girl.
And the colour ?	Green.		
Colour ?	Tartan.	Here is a —?	A boy.

Here is a simple code for telling playing cards :

For the suits :

Suit ?	Hearts.
The suit ?	Spades.
Which suit ?	Diamonds.
What suit ?	Clubs.

The numerical code must be used for the numbers of the cards ; and for the court cards :

Value ?	King.
The value ?	Queen.
What value ?	Knave.

Although we have here given only a few codes, the possibilities can be easily seen. The performers should constantly rehearse until perfect in their business.

Can you hear me ?

HOW TO MAKE A SIMPLE TELEPHONE

FIRST procure two tin cans about three inches in diameter. Take off the lids and carefully remove the bottoms, then get some parchment, or cartridge paper, and cut out two circular pieces about four inches in diameter. Bend them over the edges of the can and stick them down with seccotine, or fit a metal ring (the rim of the discarded lid will do) over the tin so that the parchment can be stretched as tight as possible. It must be taut and sound like a drum when tapped with the finger.

Next make a tiny hole in the centre of each drum and push one end of a thread of crochet cotton through ; tie a knot so that it will not come out again. The thread can be twenty to forty feet long ; it must be kept taut between the two cans, taking care that it does not come into contact with any solid object.

The vibrations of one diaphragm can then be communicated mechanically to the other, as shown in the illustration.

THE PENNY PUZZLE

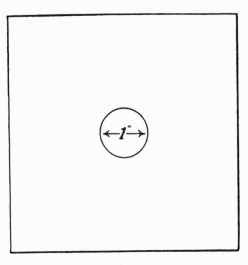

Fig. 1

TAKE a small square piece of fairly stout paper, say about four inches square, and in it cut a circular hole (see Figure 1), which is exactly one inch in diameter.

Next take an ordinary penny and you will find that it has a diameter of $1\frac{3}{16}$ inches and is thus clearly too large to go through the hole which you have cut in the square piece of paper.

Nevertheless, the puzzle is to pass the penny through the hole without tearing the paper.

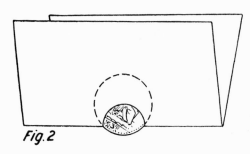

Fig. 2

Now if you look at Figure 2, you will see that the paper has been folded across the centre of the hole, and the penny dropped into the fold so that it rests in the hole, but still will not pass through. The dotted circle, of course, indicates the full size of the penny.

Next catch hold of the lower corners of the paper and slowly and gently force them up in the directions of the arrows as shown in Figure 3.

The paper will buckle in the centre and the coin will then easily fall through the hole.

It is interesting to puzzle out for yourself exactly why it will do so.

The last figure clearly indicates what actually takes place.

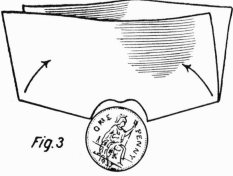

Fig. 3

WHAT ANIMAL IS THIS?

Here are eight of the most unusual but distinctive looking creatures in the world. Can you name them? Their names appear on page 118.

WHAT ANIMAL IS THIS?

Names of the Animals drawn on page 117.

Giant Panda   Ant-bear
Armadillo   (African Aardvark)
Tapir   Fennec Fox
Okapi   Kudu

Koala (Australian Native Bear)

HOW TO MAKE A PAPER TREE

TAKE a long narrow strip of paper and roll it up tightly into a cylinder as in Figure 1, sticking down the free end with gum or paste.   Then, by tearing, or with a knife or scissors, make three

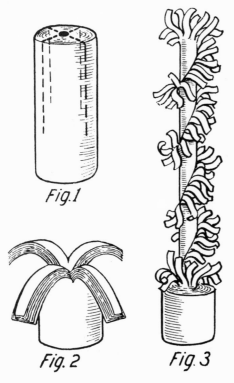

Fig. 1

Fig. 2

Fig. 3

or four incisions or cuts (see Figure 1) partly down the length of the cylinder as indicated by the dotted lines, and placing the finger at the centre of the roll, bend out the cut portions (Figure 2).   The centre of the roll is then grasped with the thumb and forefinger, or with a pair of fine-nosed pliers, and drawn out and upward to give the tree shown in Figure 3.

For reasons of realism it is obviously best to use green paper for rolling the cylinder so that the " leaves " are of an appropriate colour, and preferably the cylinder should be given an outer covering of terra-cotta red paper to simulate a flower-pot in the finished article.

PARTY GAMES

ADVERBS

ONE of the players, who later becomes the Questioner, withdraws from the group whilst the others hold their consultation. They fix upon an adverb, which they will indicate by the manner in which they answer the questions put to them. Suppose they have chosen "sarcastically," each player on being questioned, must answer in a sarcastic manner. When the Questioner has guessed the adverb, another player takes a turn. The next adverb might be "joyously," the next "briefly," then "dramatically," "disagreeably," "untruthfully," "shyly" and so on. Sometimes the demeanour of the players will indicate the word and sometimes, as in the case of "untruthfully" the actual wording of the answers. There is scope for much variety in this game.

IN THE CHOSEN MANNER

Here is a variation of the game of "Adverbs." The player who has been out of the room while the word has been selected now asks the first in the circle a question such as, "Will you draw back the curtain *in the chosen manner*?" The player then proceeds to perform the action in a way that will illustrate the adverb. The next might be asked, "Will you offer your chair to Miss Jones *in the chosen manner*?" This proceeds until the word is guessed. It will be obvious that the adverb chosen must be something that admits of dramatic interpretation.

PERSONAL REMARKS

When the players are well-known to one another great fun can be had with this game. A pack of cards is distributed. If there are fewer than twenty-six present, some of the cards should be taken out, as it is sufficient for players to have two each.

The M.C. holds on his knee a corresponding pack. He makes a personal remark or asks a question, at the same time turning up one of his cards. The player who holds the corresponding card throws it on the floor, and the remark is taken to apply to him. He then carries on the game by making another personal remark, the M.C. turns up a card, and the player with the corresponding card throws it down, and in turn makes a remark, and so on.

PARTY GAMES

" WHAT WOULD YOU DO IF——? "

There is no restriction as to the number of players in this game, but as one must act as the Questioner, he will probably be happier if he has to deal with not more than a dozen or so.

The Questioner must withdraw, and get busy thinking out a series of questions that relate to some emergency. Each question must begin with : " What would you do if——? "

The rest of the players think about mishaps, adventures, and accidents, and each having imagined himself in a particular situation, whispers his solution to his left-hand neighbour.

Thus each player is left thinking simply of one thing—the solution he has been given by his neighbour, such as " I should 'phone for the police," " I should throw it in the river," and so on.

Now the Questioner appears and asks each player in turn : " What would you do if——? " The ready-made answers must be given.

MUSICAL PARTNERS

For this game single chairs are placed, well spaced, about the room. Each boy player sits on a chair, with his partner by his side. There is a pair of players in excess of the number of chairs. When the music starts, they walk in and out of the chairs, and, when it stops, the boy sits down and takes his partner on his knee. The pair failing to find a chair drop out and a chair is removed.

MUSICAL PARTNERS (Another Way).

The arrangement is the same as in the last game except that the boy is blindfolded, and is led round by his partner, who, when the music stops, conducts him to a chair, places him on it and seats herself on his knee.

HIGH STEPPERS

The chairs are arranged in pairs but with seats together—front of seats touching front of seat. They must be in an even line round the room, and players march along in pairs, stepping on to and over the chairs as they come to them. When the music stops, any pairs of players who are partly on the chairs at the moment are eliminated and their chairs removed.

PARTY GAMES

MUSICAL MATS

A large mat should be placed at each end of the room. Players march or dance round the room (singly or in pairs) and those found stepping on the mats at the moment the music stops are eliminated.

For a slight variation of this game, draw a number of " mats " on the floor with chalk. The elimination is thus speeded up.

MUSICAL LOLLIPOP

A bar of " rock " is made up into a strong parcel, tied with ribbon or string. Secure a piece of wooden stick exactly the same length, and tie this up so that it looks exactly the same as the other parcel. These two parcels are passed in opposite directions round the circle, and, when the music stops, the players holding them drop out. The game finishes with the last two players passing the real lollipop and the dummy backwards and forwards until the music stops, whereupon they open their parcels.

MUSICAL PARCEL

A very small gift is wrapped in a very large parcel, with many separate sheets of different coloured papers, each tied with string. Players are seated in a circle, and, when the music stops, the player holding the parcel begins to unwrap it. Immediately the music continues he must relinquish it. Finally, the player who gets off the last wrapping and discloses the gift is the recipient of it.

THE MYSTERY PARCEL

A small gift is wrapped in a large parcel as in " Musical Parcel," but on each wrapping is written an instruction. When the music stops, the player holding the parcel reads aloud the message and proceeds to carry it out. Here are some examples : " Hand to the person with the nicest smile." " Hand to the guest with the biggest feet." If thought desirable, the *last* message can be : " Hand to the pianist," or " Hand to the youngest person present." It may be appropriate to single out some other guest for the special privilege of retaining the gift.

Another way of using this parcel idea is to let it follow on another game. Present the parcel to the winner of the game, and tell him (or her) to read and follow the instructions. It is handed on as before, but without music being played. The final instruction is: " Hand to the original winner," and this gives it back to the player with whom it started.

MUSICAL BOX-LIDS

Place at intervals upon the floor a number of cardboard box-lids (or pieces of cardboard) of various sizes. Players walk round, single file, while the music is played. When it stops, they must all try to crowd on to the box-lids, even standing on one foot if necessary. All players touching the ground must withdraw, and a lid is removed at each round. It is well to finish the game by having two players walking round one small lid.

MUSICAL MOTOR-PARTS

For this game write on postcards, in block letters, such words as BODY, WHEEL, SPRINGS, LAMP, ENGINE, DOOR, MASCOT, etc. Write one word on each card and have as many sets of cards as there are players. Cut the postcards in halves and mix the cards, face downwards, in a box.

The players are seated in a circle. Hand the box round the circle while the music is played. Each player in turn takes a card. When the music stops, the box is still passed round but no card is taken out until the music resumes. Unwanted cards are returned, face downwards, to the box. The first player to get a complete motor part is the winner.

PASSING THE COUNTERS

For this game competitors stand in two rows, facing one another. On a chair at each end, ten counters are placed. These are picked up one at a time by the end player and passed along the line, *right hands* only being used. When a counter reaches the end of the line, it is returned *behind* the players, by the use of the left hands only. A non-player stands at the end to receive the counters on their return journey, and the side that first gets the ten counters back is the winner.

PARTY GAMES

CHAIN MAKING

Seat the players in a circle.   The first is asked to give the name of a Town.   The second has to give a name beginning with the last letter of the previous town.   For example, first player says Brighto*n*, the second Nottingha*m*, the third Manchester.   The game gets more difficult as it proceeds, as no town must be repeated.   A player defaulting three times withdraws.   Then, by way of a change, begin a Flower chain, a Fruit chain, an Animal chain, and so on.

An interesting variation is to make a Syllable chain, each word beginning with the last syllable of the previous one, e.g. tem-per, per-son, sonnet.   Only the sounds count, and not the spelling.

This game can be made a writing one, each player compiling his own list, and the one that produces the longest list in the space of ten minutes being the winner.

THE FARMYARD

To make a success of this game the leader must be able to make up an amusing story.   Each player takes the name of a farmyard animal ; if the names run short, two players can have the same one.   The leader begins telling a story and mentioning the names of the different animals.   Each time a name is mentioned, the player must make the sound of his animal.   If he fails to do so, a point is counted against him.   Every time the leader mentions the " farmyard," all the players make their noises together.

JUMBLED WORDS

The disentangling of words that have the letters jumbled holds a fascination for most people, and there are various ways in which this idea can be utilised.

The simplest way is to compile a set of names of a class of objects, *jumble them*, and exhibit them, say, in half dozens round the room.   They should be written in block letters.   Useful groups are : birds, insects, trees, rivers, countries, girls' or boys' names, minerals, tools, things seen in a drawing room, in a garden, in a railway station, in a particular shop, etc.

PARTY GAMES

An idea for a small circle of players is to imagine that the contents of a boy's pocket has been turned out on the floor. Write the names of the articles (jumbled) on good-sized cards and place them on the floor in the midst of the players.

Write the names of books (not too well-known) and the authors' names below them, these being jumbled. A number of separate slips can be used (each bearing book and author) to be pinned on to the players, who go about guessing one another's authors. The same thing can be done with plays, poems, pictures, inventions, etc.

COUNTIES AND TOWNS

For this game players are divided into two lines, facing one another seated. A player from one side throws a rubber ball (or other small object) into the lap of a player on the other side, at the same time mentioning the name of a town. The player indicated must, before ten can be counted, give the name of the county in which the town is situated. If he succeeds, he takes the next turn and his side scores a point.

WORD MAKING

In this game competitors in turn are given a letter, and have to say as many words as they can beginning with that letter, in the space of one minute. It should be stated at the outset that derivatives are not allowed, as they are difficult to keep track of; in other words, players must not say, for example, " speak, speaker, speaking, spoke, spoken . . ." Proper names also are excepted.

RINGING THE BOTTLE

Tie a curtain ring to a piece of string and the string to a rod or walking stick. Place a bottle on the floor and let competitors endeavour to get the ring over the neck of the bottle.

MODELS MADE FROM MATCHBOXES

EMPTY matchboxes, so often thrown away as useless, form wonderful material for hundreds of toys and models. Here are a few examples that will serve to show the variety of useful objects that can be made with these handy little boxes.

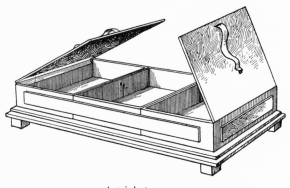

A trinket case.

A CHEST OF DRAWERS

First the boot-button knobs are put in the ends of the six matchboxes and the boxes are then seccotined together in a nest of six. The sides, bottom, top and back are covered with cardboard and two inner cases, divided and seccotined to the top as shown. Four feet are cut out of wood and fixed underneath at the corners. The whole is then enamelled. In this chest of drawers may be kept buttons, stamps, pins, etc.

A chest of drawers.

A TRINKET CASKET

The four sides are built up of matchbox cases; the bottom, partitions and lids are of cardboard. The hinges of the lids are strips of linen seccotined on to the outside ends, and the feet are four small pieces of square wood. The whole casket should be enamelled a suitable colour.

A MATCHBOX BRACKET

This bracket is made from four inner cases of matchboxes and some cardboard. The size of the cardboard frame will depend upon the size of the matchboxes you use, but it is made in one piece, with the exception of the two dividing pieces. You will find it best to make the inner structure first, and then fit in the matchboxes and matchbox trays and the partitions afterwards. With the bracket shown in the picture, four complete matchboxes are used, the front portion of each of which should be covered with leatherette paper. The " handles " (knobs) are boot buttons thrust through

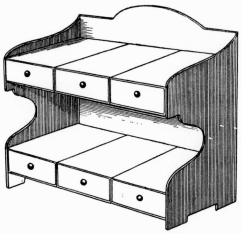

Six-drawer matchbox bracket.

from the front, with a little piece of match stalk thrust through the shank to keep them in position. Take these four boxes and then rule and cut out the two partitions and seccotine the boxes to the partitions. This gives the centre structure. Now take four inner trays of matchboxes and cover with leatherette paper ; seccotine the short ends on to the other side of the partitions and you have the entire centre structure. Then take a large piece of cardboard, place the structure in the centre and rule off the two sides and the top and bottom and cut out. Score down the two side pieces and bend them over

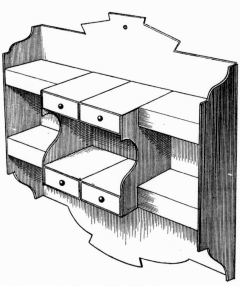

A matchbox bracket.

inwards. Seccotine the back and outer sides of the four trays and fix them to the outer cardboard structure and you have a smart little ornament which is useful as a stamp or button cabinet. The whole bracket should be enamelled white or blue, except the ends of the boxes which have been covered with leatherette paper.

The same instructions are followed for the next illustration, only here you use six complete matchboxes.

LEARNING TO SERVE.   [*Fox Photos.*

TENNIS TIPS

THE boy whose parents can afford to put him into the hands of a good coach will be amazed at the invaluable hints he can pick up. The following suggestions are those of an important County coach, and there is no doubt that you will find them very useful to you. Certainly they will improve your game.

THE SERVICE

Throw the ball high. Unless you do this your service cannot be fast. Hit the ball hard and try to direct the ball so that it clears the net by just a fraction of an inch.

Many players simply cannot produce a fast service. In their case they learn to place the ball, and it is a pleasure to watch such a player catch his opponent on the wrong foot by putting the ball in that part of the court where it was never expected.

It is a foolish habit of many players to crash over the first ball of the service in the hope that it will go into the court, and then

127

follow it by the softest possible shot because it *must* go in or count as 15 against. Such a shot is easily returned—probably an unreturnable !

Aim always for consistency. Imagine that you have only one chance, not two, and be as careful with the first ball as you will be with the second if the other one hits the net or goes out.

HITTING ON THE RISE

Why is it that some players can smash the ball back deep and others merely lift it over the net, asking for it to come back as an unstoppable shot ? The secret of fast returns is always to hit the ball *on the rise*, and *never* on the drop !

For example, A sends the ball over to B. The ball bounces. Before it reaches the top of the bounce B should smash it back as near the top of the net as possible. If B waits until the ball reaches the top of its rise and begins to fall, he cannot return the ball with the same speed. Try this yourself and see what a difference it makes when you hit the ball *on the rise*. Not only will you have the satisfaction of sending the ball back good and hard, but you are more likely to take your opponent by surprise. In any case, the ball will probably drop deep into court or even on to his base line and prevent him from attacking you.

[*Fox Photos.*

THE COACH EXPLAINS THE BACK-HAND STROKE.

THE BACKGROUND.

HOW TO MAKE A MODEL FARM

THERE is plenty of scope for imagination and the use of artistic talent in the making of a small farm scene to be used with the very realistic toys now found in the large stores. From odd lids and cartons collected from shops you can make a farm as large or as small as you wish.

To get a really effective scene, I suggest you make up a background from lids of large boxes. You can often get these from the draper. If you strengthen these lids with strips of plaster lath at the back, they will hold up firmly and will always keep their shape. Plan on these the distant hills and tiny groups, with perhaps the village church in the distance. Shade your hills so that they get darker as they near the base. The sky can be put in with shades of blue and green and with white, billowy clouds. Hills should be painted blue in the distance and the hedges can be picked out in darker green.

Separate tree groups will be useful if made 12 inches high and anything up to 12 inches long. If these are planned on the strips near the edges of boxes the part forming the lid flap will make a splendid support, as shown in the illustration. Cut out spaces in the foliage and show the boughs going through the upper sections of

the trees. This will
avoid that "solid"
look which one
would otherwise
get. The quaint
old barn or cow-
shed will be an
attraction and
should be planned
into the base of
the trees. If you
cut out the spaces

Group comprising the old barn and the trees.

for the doors, you will then be able to place animals through the space as though actually in a proper shelter. Paint the roof with thick, flat paint in fawn, ochre, light brown or tan. If you possess all these shades, then by all means, put on streaks of all of them.

The very simple little bridge shown in the illustration can be made up from any odd bits of cardboard. Such pieces of scenery are ideal for the farm where you may choose to put in a " stream." Do not cut out the fence bars but leave them in and pick out with white poster colour. A thin wash of creamy-white will suffice for the groundwork of the brickwork. Lightly mark in the walls without making them too defined. Two tree clumps on the ends will help to finish the bridge off.

Haystacks are not easy to make. I made mine up from a small carton which once held a half-pound of lard and some of those little cartons of triangular shape which contain small cheeses. As shown in the sketch the packet is sealed up firmly and stood on its side and the two tiny cartons are stood on top. To make the haystack you must next put on a thin layer of plasticine. This can be obtained from handicraft shops, and will adhere to cardboard quite well. Before the plaster is set, it can be scratched down with a comb to give the impression of hay. Mix up some thick paint in yellow, fawn, brown, etc., and apply in uneven strokes. Do not put on too much, and do not let it get through to the cardboard. With this very inexpensive process one can make quite a good array of haystacks.

The Dairy can be made easily from a long soap carton. Fix this up, just as it was when you had it from the shop. You will be able to cut out the windows with small manicure scissors. There would be no need to fill the windows in again as they are mostly open in these sheds. Make the roof from a strip of cardboard and allow this to project over each end by half an inch. Supporting gables can be made to fit on each end, and in these should be cut the doors. Paint the finished shed in dull shades of mixed fawn, yellow, cream or oddments of light-coloured paints. You will find the more varied and rough the application of these paints, the happier the result. Pick out the roof in brown, with slight uneven streaks going downwards. This model should have a long ventilator along the top. This is shown quite clearly in the sketch, and should be painted white with black strokes along each side.

The Farmhouse can be found practically ready made if you use a box about 8 inches by 8 inches and 6 inches high. I have used boxes which had four flaps for the top. If you can get one of these, you can then slope the four sections up for the roof (as shown in sketch) and thus prevent the trouble of putting on the sloping roof on gables. If used as suggested, these flaps not only make the roof but the parts to be turned down will fasten over to the side pieces and make the roof much firmer. Whilst dealing with the roof, one feels that the quaint old Dormer window might add beauty to this model. These can be made very well by the use of small cartons such as those in which small jars of medicine or meat extracts are packed. If cut to shape as shown in the illustration, they can be pasted on the roof, and with the aid of a small triangular carton the correct shape can be obtained. If unable to use the triangular shape, the best way to build the window up is to use a shaped piece of cardboard back and front to make the gables for the roof.

The Bridge.

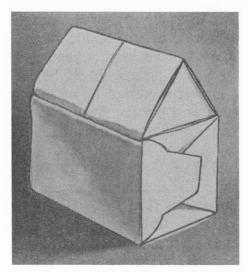

Cardboard basis for the haystack.

Provide these two pieces with flaps to fasten on to the roof section.

If you intend this to be a thatched farmhouse, then apply the plasticine as you did on the haystacks. Allow it to overhang a little to give the impression of depth. The same system of marking and painting can be applied as in the haystacks.

In a model such as this it would be best to plan up the windows on strips of cardboard and then, when drawn and suitably coloured, paste them on to the house. By this means, the traditional shutters can be worked in with the windows and frames at the same time. If your box is strong enough, you can take out the windows and re-line with various colours of toffee papers. Shutters should then be drawn on bits of cardboard and applied afterwards. Make the door central and paint it in a bright poster shade. The covering for the walls of the house should be really " Old-World " to give the right effect. Perhaps the best suggestion would be silver sand on thin glue. Another appropriate method might be the use of a mixture of sand, plaster, broken brick, etc. Flowers can be represented by groups of highly-coloured blobs on the walls, together with green foliage. These can always be added after the sand has been applied.

Chimney stacks can be made up from blocks of

The Dairy

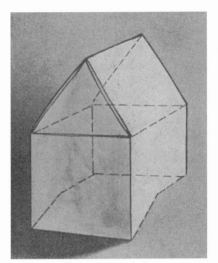

The Dormer window.

wood cut with a slit to fit on the roof. Stacks should be made from pieces of tiny dowel bar, cut into lengths of three-quarters of an inch and paint a dull red.

A simple porch can be made up as shown in the illustration, and will give a very attractive finish to the model.

Bushes, trees and other foliage can always be made from oddments of sponge dipped into your various green paints. Ornamental bushes can be made up like this and popped into the holes in the middles of cotton reels. If you paint these reels black, they will make very effective garden ornaments. Pieces of broken brick

THE PORCH.
A simple porch can be made up from a small soap carton or box of similar size. The doorway, also the windows in the two narrow sides, may be cut out with small scissors. A piece of thick cardboard will provide a flat top.

and virginia cork will make ideal rockery effects, whilst the village pond can always be made up by using a piece of that crinkled glass which we often see in windows. Most glass dealers have oddments which they will willingly give to you, if you ask them.

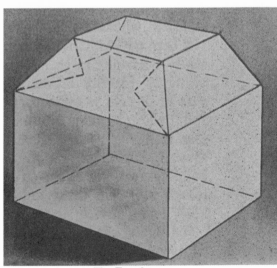

The Farmhouse.

OUT-OF-DOORS.
III

WHAT TO LOOK FOR IN AUTUMN

The Barn Owl.

AUTUMN is a wonderful time for rambles. Life is even more active than it was during the hot summer days, and all the young creatures are now fully grown and able to take their own place in Nature's scheme.

After the silence of July and August bird song begins again, and there are other interesting sounds seldom heard at any other time. The owls are noisy now. In the evenings you will hear the only owl that actually hoots—the brown or tawny owl—" Hoo-hoo-hoohoo-oooo," followed, per-haps, by the "kewick, kewick" of the female and young. By looking carefully among the large old trees in woods and parks you may often see a tawny owl perched high up, quite still, with half-closed eyes. The barn owl, which is unfortu-nately becoming rarer, largely owing to scarcity of nesting sites in the old wooden barns and buildings, may often be seen in daylight flying silently around the trees or farm buildings seeking mice. The reason why owls fly so noise-lessly is because of the enor-mous mass of soft feathers with which they are covered. The barn owl's cry is a shriek.

A Little Owl.

A DANGEROUS VISITOR.

Another owl seen in the daytime, perhaps more often than any other, is the little owl, smallest of the family.

By stream and rapid river an active bird will be seen, bobbing about in the shallows, perhaps diving underneath for quite a time, and never still. It is the dipper, black with a beautiful white breast, and it can even walk under the water in search of insects and water life, although its feet are not webbed. You may also be lucky enough to see a heron, that long-legged fisherman, grey and crested, which stands motionless waiting for some unwary fish or rat to swim near. People often say: "Look, there's a stork," when they see it, but the latter is an extremely rare visitor here.

The Tawny Owl.

Autumn is a grand time for toadstools, and thousands of different kinds wait to be discovered. Most people think of them as dangerous things and of no interest, but when one begins to know something about them, there are plenty of surprises in store. Few are really poisonous, many are eatable, but it is wisest for the beginner to leave them where they stand. Toadstools do a lot of useful work in feeding on decaying matter such as rotten wood and dead leaves. Do you know the lovely fly agaric, bright red, with white flakes, found wherever there are birch trees and bracken? This is certainly a highly-poisonous plant, but of interest when we learn that its juices were once used in making fly-papers.

On the birch trees themselves we shall see the polypore, a very

THE DIPPER.

THE HERON.
Silent and motionless he stands and awaits the approach of the unsuspecting water-rat.

hard, tough fungus which saps the life of the tree. This toadstool was once cut in slices, dried, and used as razor strops ! Then there is the morel, a grey sponge-like kind, which, in spite of its uninviting appear-

Morel.

Pixie cups.

ance, is eaten by the fungus-lover. On the Continent many kinds which we scorn are gathered and eaten, while others are dried for winter use. A fungus hunt is full of interest, and every colour from pure white to purple, green, blue, brown and black may be found.

The lichens which grow on tree trunks, old stone walls, and even on the ground are very beautiful when examined closely. See if you can find the pixie-cup, one of the prettiest kinds. Then there is "old man's beard" which grows thickly from dying tree limbs.

Brightly-coloured black and orange beetles will be busy burying the carcase of some dead mouse or bird. These are Nature's scavengers, and they lay their eggs in the body so that the grubs when hatched will have plenty of food. They are extremely interesting to watch as they systematically excavate the ground underneath the dead bird or animal and ultimately bury it entirely.

Birch polypore and fly agaric.

Look out, too, for the oak eggar, a brown moth which sends out wireless messages ! That may sound almost untrue, but if you capture a female (which has thinner " feelers " or antennæ than the male) which has just emerged from a chrysalis and put it in a box or release it in a room at home, you will soon discover males flying around seeking her *although there may not have been any for a mile.*

How she broadcasts is one of the mysteries of Nature that have never been solved. The antennæ of the male are more elaborate and more sensitive than those of the female, and male moths have been known to come from a distance of two to three miles. Some naturalists contend this is due to a wonderfully keen scent.

When a quick, brown animal streaks across your path you often ask : '' Is that a stoat or a weasel ? ''

It is really quite easy to tell the difference between a stoat and a weasel. Size alone is usually a deciding factor, the stoat being a much larger animal than the weasel and in most places much more common.

The oak eggar moth.

The weasel is one of the smallest carnivoræ found in Great Britain. It is brown in colour with more or less white on the middle of the belly and has a short tail, only about two inches long, the head and body measuring six or seven inches. The stoat, as we have already stated, is considerably larger, the head and body measuring about eleven inches, and the tail five. The most distinctive feature is the tip

Burying beetles.

of the tail, which in the stoat is black, otherwise the colouring of the two animals is almost identical, so look out for the black tail tip and you will have no difficulty in distinguishing between Mr. Weasel and Mr. Stoat, except, of course, in winter, when they turn completely white.

Then size must be your guide.

A stoat.

TOYS MADE WITH MATCHES

MANY toys and interesting models can be made with matches. Most of the furniture for a doll's house can be easily constructed and here we show how some of the articles can be made. Lack of space will not allow of instructions for making anything like a complete set, but the reader can easily elaborate and invent for himself.

All that is required is some seccotine, a quantity of the largest size matches, and some " doll's pins." (Messrs. Bryant and May sell match-sticks free of igniting material specially for toy-making.)

A model of a doll's bedstead is seen in Figure 4. This is made up of two sides and two ends. The head end is shown in Figure 1. The two upright match-sticks a have four cross-sticks b let into them. Before these are fixed, however, the narrow upright bars c (cut from " Swan " vestas) are glued in position. The complete end is then glued together, with the top cross-stick d and the little intermediate bar e added.

The foot end of the cot is the same as the head, except that the upright sticks a are about a quarter of an inch shorter and the top cross-stick d and little bar e are omitted.

The cot sides are seen in Figure 2, where x represents the head end and y the foot. The sides consist of four horizontal sticks, which are fixed to the two ends with pins. Between the two upper sticks there is a row of " Swan Vesta " bars neatly glued in position.

To form a bottom for the cot a piece of pine veneer or cardboard

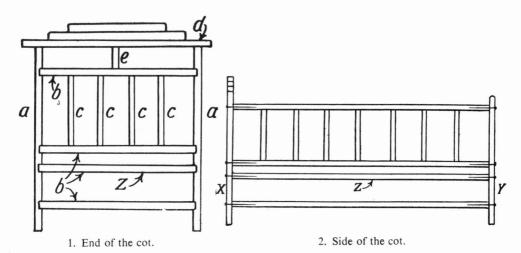

1. End of the cot. 2. Side of the cot.

141

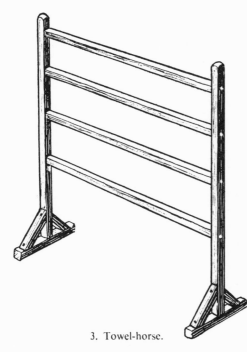

3. Towel-horse.

may be cut and fitted so that it rests on the sticks marked *z* in the figure. The corners will be cut away so that the veneer clears the four upright sticks which form the posts.

In Figure 3 is shown a model of a towel-horse.

The sides and cross bars are ordinary safety match-sticks, the cross bars slightly shortened. The feet are short pieces of matchstick.

It is fastened together entirely with tiny pins.

The illustrations in this article will give an idea of what may be achieved by ingenuity and patient labour.

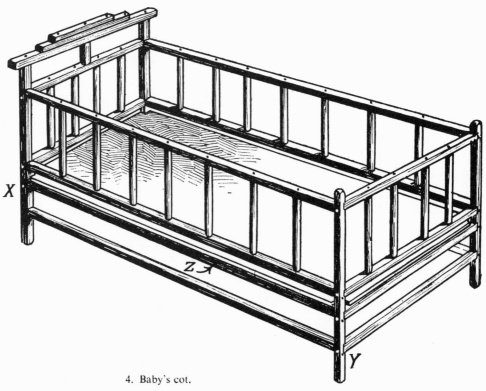

4. Baby's cot.

A CAT STALKING A RABBIT.

GETTING DOWN TO IT—STALKING

HERE'S something you have to get down to—in more ways than one !

Something that requires plenty of practice and patience—and yet something which is full of interest to all who enjoy the Open Air, to all interested in nature study and in photographing wild life.

Stalking . . .

The business of the stalker is really to approach as near to a certain objective—be it man or animal—without being seen, heard or scented by the quarry in question.

One of your first considerations must be clothing. No bright colours or shiny ornaments should be worn, and the colour of the garments should correspond as nearly as possible with the natural surroundings. Anything of a green, brown or fawn nature, therefore, is likely to be suitable if you are stalking in the country.

This alone will not serve to hide you from your quarry. You must study carefully the country between you and your objective, and decide upon a route which will afford you the maximum cover from trees, bushes, grass, hillocks, boulders, etc.—remembering that the shortest route is not always the best.

Be careful about hiding in long grass—for, though it hides you,

GETTING DOWN TO IT—STALKING

Timid creatures of
the wild are always
on the lookout for
danger.

your presence may be revealed by the waving of the grass as you
crawl through it. Guard against showing yourself on the skyline—
and similarly, when taking cover behind a rock, or tree-stump, do
not risk detection by showing your head over the top : Look round
the side if you wish to make any observations.

When you are close to the animal, or whatever you are stalking,
you can often remain hidden by adopting some simple camouflage,
such as the holding of a leafy branch in front of you, or the placing
of leaves or twigs in your hat or parts of your clothing. Should the
animal chance to look up, or become suspicious, you will then be
less conspicuous against the natural surroundings, *provided you keep
perfectly still.*

This last remark leads us to another important point : the
ability to walk quietly, and to freeze—that is, stand perfectly rigid
just where you are—on the instant when necessary.

This needs a great deal of practice, but it can be done—and care
must be taken to see that you do not, while moving along, cause
twigs to crack underfoot, or leaves to rustle at your side. Carefully

lift aside any branch or bush which you have to pass, and watch out for stones, bumps in the ground, and tree roots. A fall—or even a stumble—will create such a noise that will more than probably scare all wild life from the neighbourhood.

You will not be able to approach very close to some of the sharp-eyed and sharp-eared animals and birds if you remain on your feet. At a certain distance (which you will find out with practice) it becomes necessary to " get down to it," crouching lower and lower the nearer you approach, until you end up by crawling. Never be tempted to rush or hurry over the last few yards. " Slow and steady " wins every time.

For success in the final crawling stage, you cannot do better than follow the oft-given advice : Watch a cat. If you can only study the movements of a cat when stalking, and imitate them as nearly as possible, you will be well on the way to becoming a good stalker.

One final matter to be considered in the actual method of approach is the sense of smell—much greater in animals than in men, and greater in some animals than others. In this way your quarry may detect your approach, however careful and quiet you may have been.

[Sport & General.

A SETTER " FREEZING."

GETTING DOWN TO IT—STALKING

You can avoid this in large measure by studying the direction of the wind, and making sure that you stalk *against* it. If the wind is blowing from the animal towards you, the chances of your being scented are considerably reduced, especially if the wind is strong.

*   *   *

All this may seem a lot of preparation for the enjoyment of stalking, but it is worth it—while, apart from its use when mastered in outdoor scouting games, the very practising of it is in itself an absorbing activity.

Those who study nature and wild life have their reward when they are able to watch their favourite birds and animals in their natural surroundings, photographing them from some suitably-placed hideout, and taking note of their colour, form, habits, peculiarities, or whatever your particular interest in them happens to be.

That is the real fun of stalking—to join battle, as it were, with Nature on her own ground . . . with " close-ups " of her secrets as the spoils of victory.

Caught in the act by a patient stalker. A Red-breasted Merganser swallowing a fish.

146

[Fox Photos.

THE 80-YARD SPRINT FOR THE " UNDER-FOURTEENS."

ATHLETICS—A FINE SPORT

SPRINTING

IN races up to 440 yards, where speed is all-important, you cannot have too much practice. Do not practise on your own however ; you must have a companion. And if he is a little faster than you are at the beginning, so much the better. Do not practise too assiduously or you will be stale before the day of the sports.

In the 100-yards race split-seconds count. Learn to get off the mark quickly. If you are a tenth of a second behind an opponent, he may hold that lead throughout. Remember that the race is over almost as soon as it is started, and there is not much difference between good men. One good starting tip for you is this—on the pistol shot do not rise to your full height *immediately*. Rise in a sort of diagonal movement. The quicker you come up to normal stance, the slower your speed at the commencement.

ATHLETICS—A FINE SPORT

The 440-yards race requires pace and stamina above all else. In practice you should run at full speed over half the distance, gradually increasing 20 or 40 yards at a time. In this way you will gradually work up a high speed for the whole of the distance. If you train by running a fast 440 yards all the time, you will take too much out of yourself.

ONE MILE

Staying power rather than speed is necessary for this race, and again in your practice it is advisable to do your fast work up to three-quarters of a mile only, at the beginning. When you feel that you can tackle the mile at speed, run against the stop watch and keep careful note of your time. Do not overdo time trials.

HURDLES

These are often of 120-yards distance with ten hurdles, each ten yards apart. In your practice you should try to take the hurdles in your stride so that, as the foot comes down to the ground, it is always ready to push the body forward on to the other foot for the next stride. You should practise with the hurdles the correct distance apart, otherwise in the race you may find yourself being baulked by reaching the hurdles either before or after you are ready for them.

JUMPING

If you are training for the high jump, you will have to get rid of superfluous muscle in the leg. The question of the run to take before making the jump is a matter for careful consideration. You may find that eight, ten or twelve paces may be your ideal. Timing the take-off is a great art and needs plenty of practice. When you take the jump, tuck in your legs and throw your body forward and upward with every ounce of strength you possess.

LONG JUMPING

Here again you must time your steps very carefully in order to arrive at the jump ready for the take-off. It is useless reaching the jump half-way between a stride. In such a case, obviously, much of the impetus created by the run will be wasted. Long jumping is a fascinating event and one in which the average boy can be very successful.

ATHLETICS—A FINE SPORT

GENERAL TRAINING HINTS

It is essential that you have good food and plenty of sleep—nine hours each night for preference. You must, of course, practise the events in which you are taking part as often as possible, but in moderation. Don't keep on until you are sick of the event, and the novelty has worn off.

[Fox Photos.

"FLYING" THE HURDLES.

So far as food is concerned, cut out all pastry during training. Do not exercise too strenuously first thing in the morning before you have had breakfast.

You should have a daily cold bath and a good rub down.

After practice wrap yourself up so that you are warm, otherwise you may easily get a chill. Don't stand about talking after practice before you have thrown on a scarf or sweater.

On the day of the race avoid heavy meals and do not drink too much water.

CIPHERS AND CODES

THERE are hundreds of ways in which you may write to a friend by means of a cipher, or writing which only the possessor of the key can read.

It is only necessary to decide upon signs to represent letters and write your message by means of these signs. Such signs may be other letters: for example, you might write the alphabet out as follows and place other letters under :—

A B C D E F G H I J K L M N O P Q R S T U V W X Y Z
D X I Q A K J L M R E V T P U C G F H W O N Z Y B S

Then when writing a message, you simply use the letter in the under line for the letter in the upper line. Thus, if you wished to write " How are you ? " you would take the letter under H for H, and the letter under O for O and so on, so that your message would be written thus : LUZDFABUO ? Your friend, having the key, which is the alphabet arranged as we have shown, simply looks for the letter above L and finds it is H and then the letter above U and finds it is O and the letter above Z, and so gets " How " and so on.

Another simple but baffling cipher is possible by writing a quantity of letters, only some of which are to be regarded. For example, you have an arrangement with your chum that when you write, only the second, sixth and eighth letters are to be taken into account.

The message " How are you ? " would come out like this :

B *H* Z M A *O* H *W* J *A* F L Y *R* N E M *Y* O P T *O* D U
1 2 3 4 5 6 7 8 1 2 3 4 5 6 7 8 1 2 3 4 5 6 7 8

Now your correspondent looks along the line and finds the second letter is H, the sixth letter O, the eighth W, and the next second A, and so on.

This code has the disadvantage of necessitating the use of a large number of letters. For our " How are you ? " message we have to employ twenty-four.

The Playfair Code may be used, and to code a message by this method, first draw six horizontal lines, about a quarter of an inch apart, and across these, six vertical lines, thus forming twenty-five small squares. Starting at the top left-hand corner write horizontally the code word (known to both sender and receiver of the message) letter by letter in successive squares. It is usual to choose for a code word one which does not contain the letters I or J or a repetition of the same letter : such a word as " panda " would not be suitable.

D	E	N	O	L
A	B	C	F	G
H	I	K	M	P
Q	R	S	T	U
V	W	X	Y	Z

The remaining squares are to contain the other letters of the alphabet in their correct order ; as there are only twenty-five spaces I and J are counted as the same letter, and each letter in the code word is included only once.

When this framework has been constructed, the message can be coded. First the letters of the message are ticked off in pairs, irrespective of words. Then each pair is found on the chart and note taken of the two letters forming with them the opposite corners of a rectangle. Thus in our illustration the letters X and B form, with C and W a rectangle. These two letters are those to be sent in the code message. Should the letters to be coded be either side by side or one above the other in the frame, the letters to the right or above are respectively adopted as the code. Thus " D E " would be, in code, " E N," while " Q V " would be " H Q." In decoding, of course, the reverse order is observed : instead of " to the right and up," the motto is " to the left and down."

If the message to be coded has an odd number of letters, the last pair is completed by the addition of such a letter as X or Z, which will be readily recognised by the recipient as a " fill-up " letter, and will not affect the sense of the message.

If you prefer you can write your message in the ancient Ogham alphabet. This alphabet is as follows :

So if you wished to write " Come here," you would do it thus :

Boy Scouts often leave a message on the road or in a field by an arrangement of stones, sticks, etc., placed in certain positions on

CIPHERS AND CODES

each side of a piece of string or a line drawn on the ground. Take the following arrangement as the key :

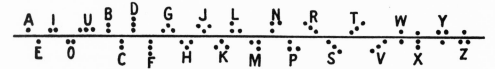

Now if you wish to leave the message, " Come here," you arrange your pebbles thus :

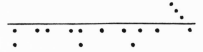

Here is another useful code. Take some form and place dots in different positions to make them represent letters. We might take the form used in the old " Noughts and Crosses " game and arrange the dots as in this diagram.

Now when we wish to write our message we just take the form in which the letter appears and put a dot in a position corresponding with that in which the letter occurs. So if we wished to write " Come here," we should do it thus :

A	.	J	.	S	.	2
B	.	K	.	T	.	3
C	.	L	.	U	.	4
D	.	M	.	V	.	5
E	.	N	.	W	.	6
F	.	O	.	X	.	7
G	.	P	.	Y	.	8
H	.	Q	.	Z	.	9
I	.	R	.	10	.	0

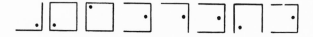

THE MORSE CODE

Perhaps the most famous of all codes is the Morse Code— Here it is :—

A · —   B — · · ·   C — · — ·   D — · ·

E ·   F · · — ·   G — — ·   H · · · ·

I · ·   J · — — —   K — · —   L · — · ·

M — —   N — ·   O — — —   P · — — ·

Q — — · —   R · — ·   S · · ·   T —

U · · —   V · · · —   W · — —   X — · · —

Y — · — —   Z — — · ·

152

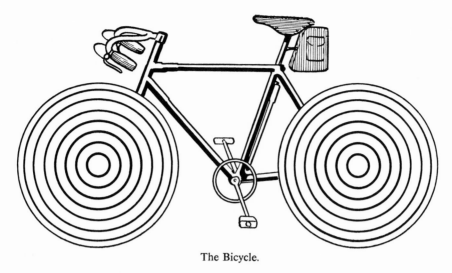

The Bicycle.

IS SEEING BELIEVING?—II

AS we have already explained in our first article on Is Seeing Believing? our eyes are apt to deceive us at times. Here is a diagram of a bicycle which illustrates the well-known optical illusion of wheels that spin round and round.

If you hold the design in your hand and give it a twirl by means of a slight circular movement of the wrist, you will apparently set the wheels of the bicycle turning round and round. The faster you move the design, the faster the bicycle seems to travel.

A reversing movement will make the wheels appear to spin in the opposite direction.

The effect is more satisfactory if we do not look too directly at the wheels.

These rotating wheel movements are particularly striking in combinations such as that represented in our next diagram, in which a multiplicity of circles does not allow us to fix our gaze definitely on any one wheel.

Here is an illusion with which you will catch the vast majority of people. Pin a large sheet of white paper against the wall, touching the floor at the bottom. Then, when no one is looking, place a dark object—a black ornament or a dart board serves very well—on the floor immediately in front of the paper as shown in the diagram.

Notice the height to which it comes on the paper and remove it before anyone sees it.

Then ask those present to come forward one by one and mark

A combination of rotating wheels.

on the paper the height to which they think the object would come. Finally, make your own mark and place the article used in position. You will find that your friends will all be a long way out, and, unless you are very careful, you will be wrong yourself !

Most of the marks will be far too high.

Borrow a silver watch, and cover the back with the tips of the first, second and third fingers of both hands. Hold the back of the watch towards the audience, gently move the watch to and fro, at the same time part and rejoin the finger tips a little. Much to the consternation of the owner of the watch and the amusement of your audience the watch will look as if it were bending.

A little trick on the eyes, which is really a most curious puzzle, is carried out in this way. Cut a piece of card which is four and a half inches long and one and three-eighths inches wide. On this draw out the figures to indicate eleven match-sticks. Now draw a diagonal line across the card, one end of which just clears the top of the first match-stick and the other the bottom of the last. Cut along the line with scissors so that the card is in two pieces. Put the two halves on the table in their original position and count the match-sticks to make sure that there are eleven. Now move the upper half of the card one stage along. Count the match-sticks and to your amazement there are now only ten. Move the upper half back again to its first position, and you will have back again the original eleven match-sticks. Few people will guess the explanation of this puzzle, which can be explained as follows. The eleventh match is really there all the time, but not as a whole. When you have cut and moved the card one stage to the left, this has the effect of dividing one of the matches into ten parts. Each of the ten matches in the arrangement is just a tenth of a match longer than it was before, but the difference is too small for your eyes to detect.

Our eyes take every opportunity of giving themselves a rest, and this results in a number of illusions. For instance, if you look very hard at a black object for a minute or two and then look away at a dark background, you will have the impression of a black object reversed in white.

Fix your gaze on the black skeleton for a few moments and then look at a dark wall-paper or surface, and the black figure will appear reversed in white on the dark background. What happens is that the constant vision of the black or white tires the part of the retina on which it falls ; so when you look at the background, the tired part refuses to be stimulated, with the result that the image appears in the reverse of what you actually saw. We also must always remember that black is not a colour, but simply the absence of all light.

It is interesting to note that optical illusions fail to deceive the eye when they are seen for the barest fraction of a second. If you arrange the illusions so that you can see them by the light of one electric spark, you will find that the various optical illusions which we have described in the two articles are no longer operative. The spark gives plenty of time for the form of the illusions, but not sufficient time for the eye to move and be deceived.

With a simple toy that anyone can make you get

How tall is this jug ?

an X-ray effect. From a piece of thin card cut a strip about six inches long and one inch wide. Half an inch from each end of the strip cut out a round hole half an inch in diameter and fold the strip of card in the centre so that these holes fall exactly one above the other. It is easier to fold the strip of card first and then remove the two round pieces of card together. Between the holes slip a white hen's feather, fix with gum and trim away flush with the top and bottom of your card strip. Now stand in front of a window and place your hand about fifteen inches from your X-ray toy, the opening of which is kept close to your nose. Move your hand backwards and forwards to get the focus, and you will soon find a position where the shadows of the bones of your hand can be distinctly seen.

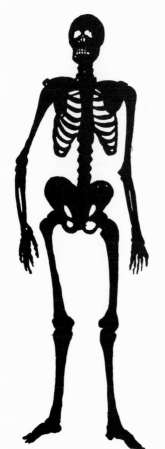

The skeleton.

LOOKING THROUGH YOUR HAND

Here is an amusing illusion with which you can deceive your friends. Prepare a tube of plain white paper, about eight inches long and one inch in diameter. Offer your friend this tube and tell him to place it to his right eye. Then get him to hold his left hand half-way down the tube and in front of his left eye, and ask him what he can see. He will see what appears to be a hole clean through the palm of his left hand, through which he can plainly see objects in the room. The explanation is of course that the right eye was seeing things through the tube over a limited compass, while the left eye was having its view blocked, and the two eyes were thus prevented from working in conjunction.

A LESSON ON KNOTS.

[*Graphic Photo Union.*

SOME USEFUL KNOTS

FEW people realise the great variety of knots in use by sailors, builders, and others. There are simple knots for rope ends, knots for joining ropes, ties and lashings, anchor and mooring fastenings, shortenings, and for various other purposes. Every boy should learn to tie some at least of them. There are many occasions when life itself depends on a knot having been properly tied. The great things to remember are that knots should be capable of bearing any kind of strain and that they should be so tied that it is easy to undo them when required. By means of the illustrations any intelligent lad can soon acquire the necessary knowledge, and elaborate directions are not needed. The knots should be practised constantly, and you will be surprised at the amount of interest they yield.

Bight of a Rope.—The bight of a rope is an unknotted loop in a rope, or it may refer to any part of a rope between the two ends.

Overhand or Thumb Knot.—This is the usual form of knot put in the end of a rope to prevent it from unreeving. The knot is formed by making a loop in the rope and passing the free end through.

SOME USEFUL KNOTS

Figure-of-eight Knot.—Another form of knot for rope ends, formed by making a loop and winding the free end once round before passing it through the loop. The simple *Flemish Knot* is similar.

Sometimes the end of a rope is finished with a *Wall Knot*, made by untwining the strands and interlocking each with the looped preceding one, passing the ends up through loops. Then work all parts well taut, whip ends of strands together and cut off short. The *Crown Knot* differs in that the free ends point downwards.

Double Knot.—The *Double Knot* is formed by passing the free end of the rope twice through the loop made as for the simple knot, and the sixfold knot is similarly made, the end being passed through the loop six times.

Sheep Shank.—To shorten ropes which require lengthening again a Sheep Shank is employed. This is made by gathering up the amount to be shortened in a loop parallel with the rope, and forming *half hitches round the two ends. The ends may then be †toggled if necessary.

Shortening Loops.—Another method of shortening ropes temporarily is by loops and turns, which are clearly illustrated and can easily be made after a little practice.

Chain.—Various decorative arrangements are in use for shortening. The principal ones are the *Chain, Double Chain* and *Double Twist.* The Chain is made of overhand knots, each one embracing the previous loop, and the double chain is of figure-of-eight knots. Good examples can be seen on halters at horse fairs.

Parbuckle.—This is used for handling casks up or down an incline where there is no crane or lifting tackle. The middle of a stout rope is placed over a post at the top of the incline and the two ends passed round the two quarters of the cask and taken to the top. The cask then lies in the U-shaped ropes and by pulling, or lowering out, together the cask can be raised or lowered on the incline.

Bowline.—A bowline is used for slinging a man over the ship's side, or for lowering from aloft. Form a small loop, then put the end of the rope through, form a large loop, and pass the end at the

---

*A half-hitch is a jamming loop made with the bight of a rope, either free or round some object. It has only slight holding effect and is invariably used in conjunction with other bends and hitches.
   †Toggle is a small piece of wood which is slipped through the bights and half-hitches to increase holding power.

SOME USEFUL KNOTS

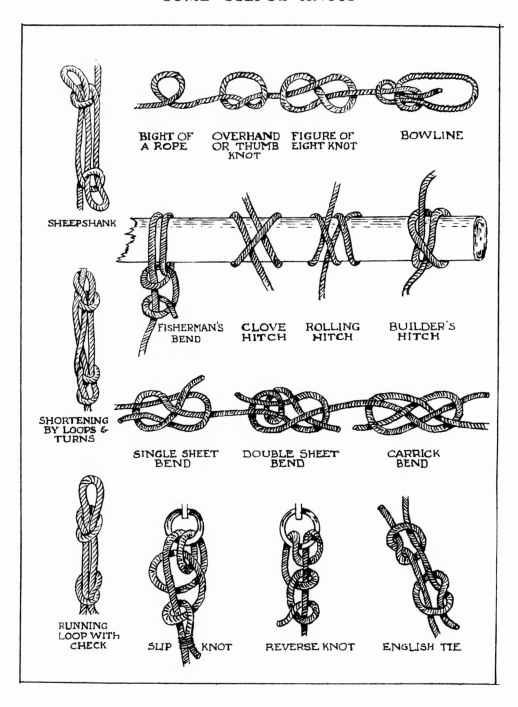

BIGHT OF A ROPE   **OVERHAND OR THUMB KNOT**   **FIGURE OF EIGHT KNOT**   **BOWLINE**

SHEEPSHANK

FISHERMAN'S BEND   **CLOVE HITCH**   **ROLLING HITCH**   **BUILDER'S HITCH**

SHORTENING BY LOOPS & TURNS

SINGLE SHEET BEND   **DOUBLE SHEET BEND**   **CARRICK BEND**

RUNNING LOOP WITH CHECK   **SLIP KNOT**   **REVERSE KNOT**   **ENGLISH TIE**

See also illustrations on page 161.

back of the standing part. Return the end through the small loop and pull tight.

A *Running Bowline* is the above arranged as a slip knot; it is used wherever a running noose is required. A *Bowline on the Bight* is formed by doubling the rope and using both parts together. Commence as for a bowline and pass the loop end over the knot.

Loop.—This is formed by doubling the rope and making an overhand knot. A *Running Loop* is made by forming a loop and making an overhand knot with the free end of the rope, so that the standing part is embraced.

A *Flemish Loop* is similar, but with a Flemish knot.

A *Running Loop with Check* is the running loop with an overhand knot in both parts of the rope.

Reserve Knot.—This is used for heavy pulls. The free end of the rope is passed round the standing part as shown in the illustration.

Ordinary Tie.—This is formed by holding the ends of both ropes and tying an ordinary overhand knot. The *Flemish Tie* is a variation in the knot and is as illustrated.

English Tie.—This is formed by making an overhand knot in each end of the ropes to be joined so that each knot embraces the standing part of the other rope. When the ropes are taut the knots butt (come together).

Reef Knot.—This is the knot generally used for joining ropes, and is made by placing the two ends over one another, forming loops, and passing the ends through as shown. Care must be taken to see that both parts of the one rope are on the same side of the loop on the other rope.

A *Granny* is incorrect, and is the result of a careless attempt to make the reef knot.

The *Weaver's Knot*, or *Sheet Bend*, is somewhat similar to the reef; it will be seen that the end of one rope is tucked under its standing part. A *Double Sheet Bend* has this end passed round the knot before it is tucked under the standing part. The sheet bend is useful when joining two ropes of unequal thickness.

The method of forming a *Carrick Bend* will be readily seen in the illustration.

A *Fisherman's Bend* is formed by taking two turns around the pole and making a half hitch, the rope end being taken under one

SOME USEFUL KNOTS

REEF   GRANNY   FLEMISH TIE

SHROUD KNOT

MARLINE SPIKE HITCH   TIMBER HITCH   HITCH WITH TWO ENDS & CHECK   SIMPLE LASHING

SAILORS KNOT

WALL KNOT (HOW IT IS TIED)   CHAIN FASTENING   DOUBLE CHAIN FASTENING

LARK'S HEAD CROSSED   SIMPLE BOAT KNOT   DELAY KNOT   CAPSTAN KNOT

See also illustrations on page 159.

of the turns. Additional security is gained by making a second half hitch as shown in our diagram.

Sailor's Knot.—This has the end of the rope carried round the standing part of two half hitches. The *Round Turn and Two Half Hitches* differ only in that the rope is carried completely round the hook ; this knot is used for securing a hawser to the ring of a buoy.

Shroud Knot.—The method of making this, as well as the *Capstan, Delay* and *Slip Knots*, will be seen by referring to the diagrams.

Simple Boat Knot.—This is a quickly detachable fastening for mooring boats, etc., and has the standing part of the rope picked through an overhand knot in the end. A *Lark's Head Crossed* is just two half hitches on a ring. A *Catspaw* is often used for attaching a rope to a hook. It is formed by making a temporary loop and throwing the doubled end back on the two ropes ; the two doubled ends thus formed are twisted up to make two eyes, into which the hook is placed.

Simple Lashing.—This is as illustrated.

Timber Hitch.—This is used for securing the end of a rope to a spar, and for bending the rope round light cases, etc. It is formed by making a half hitch with a long end of the rope and winding the end backwards upon itself.

Rolling Hitch and Clove Hitch.—These are also easily followed from the diagram. For slipping a line over a post the clove hitch is made by forming two loops on a line and doubling them back to form a single loop through which the pole is slipped.

Marline Spike Hitch.—This is formed by the standing part of the rope being picked through a loop laid over it, so that the spike lays under the standing part and over the sides of the loop. It is used for hooking the hook of tackle to any rope where a small pull is required, or for heaving the turns of a *seizing taut with a marline spike.

Builders' Hitch.—This is quickly made as illustrated and is used for supporting or lifting timber. The *Hitch with two ends and Check* can also be readily followed from the diagram.

Chain Fastening.—The formation of the *Chain Fastening* will be apparent. The arrangement of the *Double Chain Fastening* is in the form of half hitches carried alternately round the two ends of the scaffolds and is a method largely used in building operations.

---

*Seizing is a length of small stuff—marline, codline, or other small rope. It is used to secure (seize) together two parts of a larger rope so that neither shall rend under strain.

WHAT DOGS ARE THESE?
(For answers see page 166.)

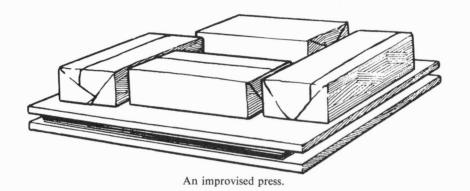

An improvised press.

PRESSING AND DRYING
FLOWERS AND PLANTS

TO start a collection of preserved plants, or a herbarium, you will need only a collecting box (a tin sandwich box, or something like it), some quires of paper of a spongy nature (blotting paper is good, Bentall's botanical paper better), two stout boards to form the top and bottom of your " press," and three or four bricks wrapped in brown paper. If you can get the use of an old-type letter-copying press you can dispense with boards and bricks. The specimens can be arranged in botanical classification or by any other method that may commend itself.

Collecting the Specimens. Collect specimens as perfect as possible, avoiding weather-damaged flowers and those partly eaten by insects. With many flowers you can collect specimens in all stages of growth, from bud to seed, and, of course, you will eventually mount all such life-history sets on single cards, devoting one card to each set. Thus a daisy would be shown in the bud, with young leaves, half-open, in full bloom, and in seed, all on the same card.

If preferred you can collect only flowers or plants of a certain class or order. If you are anything of a botanist, you will know what is meant by the order *Ranunculacæ*, or *Saxifragæ*, or *Rosaceæ*. One young friend of the writer has a unique collection of preserved medicinal plants. For years he has been collecting such plants as wild camomile, yellow gentian, valerian, yarrow, poppy, peppermint, wild marjoram, common sage, purple orchis, mullein, arnica, etc., etc.

Yet another excellent collection might be made of food plants, such as pea (blossom, stem and pod), dwarf bean, wheat, barley, potato (leaf, stem and blossom), wild strawberry, maize, oats, millet, etc. Another collection might consist entirely of ferns.

Drying and Pressing. When you have reached home with your specimens, you proceed to dry them. Place a board on the table, then four or five thicknesses of blotting paper or botanical paper, and on these your specimens, spreading out the petals, etc., with your fingers or a camel-hair brush. Having placed out the desired number (do not crowd them, and, of course, they must not overlap) place four or five sheets of paper on top, then more specimens, more paper, more specimens, and so on. The pile is then transferred to the press, if you have one ; if not, the other board is placed on top and four bricks above it.

Leave for about thirty hours, then take out all specimens carefully and put between fresh paper. Press for a further forty-eight hours.

Mounting and Labelling. Make sure that the plants or flowers are thoroughly dry before mounting them. Use your discretion as to the tint of card upon which the specimens are mounted. Many methods of fixing have been tried, but nothing is better than the old plan of small strips of stamp (gum) paper, one-eighth of an inch wide, placed across the stalk, etc. For heavy specimens a small quantity of seccotine may be used on a thick part of the flower or plant.

Every specimen should be carefully labelled, the names being written on the card itself or on separate labels. Write the generic and specific names legibly in the right-hand corner.

If the plant is small, or moderately small, the whole root included should be gathered and preserved. Stems which are too thick to be flat may be whittled down (at the back only) with a sharp knife.

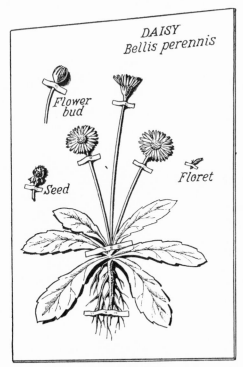

The pressed sections of a daisy arranged to show its life history.

PRESSING AND DRYING FLOWERS AND PLANTS

Preserving in Silver Sand. Yet another method of preserving flowers in their natural colours is by means of silver sand. Get a large and fairly shallow box without a lid. Knock off the bottom and, leaving it disconnected, stand the four sides of the box upon it. Now place a thin layer of clean silver sand in the box and on this lay the flowers, which must be fresh, but quite dry, and cover carefully with sand. With bell-shaped flowers, such as tulips, the inside must be filled with sand and placed mouth upwards. If the box is large enough a second layer of flowers may be added. The frame is now placed in a warm dry place (a sunny shelf of the greenhouse is best) and left for about ten days ; the flowers will then be dry and wonderfully bright and natural looking. The blooms will be rather brittle and care must be used in handling them.

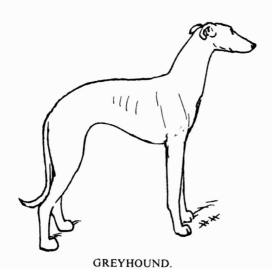

GREYHOUND.

WHAT DOGS ARE THESE ?

List of the Dogs illustrated on page 163.

Wire-haired Terrier
Labrador Retriever
Scottish Terrier
Bulldog

Great Dane
Alsatian
St. Bernard

Irish Setter
Sealyham
Cocker Spaniel
Airedale

166

YOUNG, BUT QUITE EXPERT.   [*Sport & General.*]

ROWING AND CANOEING

IT is only after watching such an academic event as the Boat
Race that one realises how poor one is on the water. Yet, as
with every other sport, the more tips you learn from watching the
experts the easier it will be for you to see where your own handling
of a boat is bad.

One of the best ways to practise, in the beginning, is to hire a
sliding-seat skiff on a park lake, and then row quietly away somewhere and set about improving your style.

A bad fault of many rowers is that of pulling more strongly with
one arm than the other. This is quite natural, because in normal life
one arm is used more than the other, and therefore even in rowing
there is a tendency to use it more powerfully. If, however, you watch
your hands as the oars are drawn inwards, you can make certain that
they work parallel with each other and not one ahead of the other.

Do not dig at the water or send the blade in obliquely. In the
latter case, the blade will sink far too deeply, so that much of the
power of the stroke is wasted.

167

Blisters are a sign that you allow the oars to move in your hands. The oars should be held firmly and all movement be made by the wrists. The art of feathering the water is quite easy to acquire. The oars are brought back to the dipping position parallel with the surface of the water, or even by " plashing " along the surface of the water.

To get every bit of power from your stroke, allow the blades of their own accord to come out of the water at the end of the pull.

CANOEING

This is not nearly so popular as normal rowing, because it is usually more difficult to manœuvre the boat. The Canadian-type canoe is propelled by a single-bladed oar which is used on one side of the boat only. A special method has to be learned in order to prevent the boat from working over at an angle.

The English-type canoe has a double-bladed oar which is dipped into the water on each side alternately. An annoyance of canoeing with a double-bladed oar is that the water continually runs along the blade and either falls into the boat or on to one's clothes.

Canoeing is really fine sport and makes an excellent holiday; but it is not advisable to take a canoe on a trip of any distance until one has mastered the art properly by constant practice.

PADDLING THEIR CANOE.   [*Sport & General.*

THE MORNING P.T. CLASS.   [*Sport & General.*

PHYSICAL EXERCISES FOR FITNESS

TO be fit to play exciting games, one must go in for healthy exercises, and here are a number that can be practised by boys and girls either out-of-doors in company with others, or indoors before an open window.

THE CROW HOP

First of all, a few leg exercises, commencing with the crow hop. Raise the heels, then bend the knees until you are almost squatting on your raised heels. In this position, take short hops forward, backward, to the left and right. The arms may be free at the beginning, but later should be placed on the knees. The body and head must be held erect.

BACK TO BACK

This is one that is principally an outdoor exercise. It is done in pairs with two boys or girls leaning against each other, back to back, with their feet in a forward position.

The exercise consists in the pair sitting on the floor and rising while keeping their backs touching. The pairs should be roughly of the same height and weight.

169

LEG EXERCISES.

Sport & General.

CROSS LEGS

Another good leg exercise is sitting down and repeatedly crossing one's legs, without using the hands. A third is the popular one of lying on the back with the hands at hips, and lifting the legs high in the air with the buttocks clear of the ground, going through the motion of cycling.

BALANCING EXERCISES

Here are two exercises to help you keep your balance. First, raise one knee to the forehead with the head bent down and touching it. Then grasp the knee firmly from in front, keep the other leg as straight as possible and count to as high a number as you can without becoming unduly tired. Repeat this with the other leg.

The second is the more difficult " thread the needle " exercise. In this the hands are clasped in front with the fingers interlocked. Then first one foot and then the other is " threaded " through the hands until both arms are behind. When this has been accomplished, the process of " unthreading " is started.

PHYSICAL EXERCISES FOR FITNESS

SIDE-BENDING EXERCISES

" Sideways passing " is as much a game as an exercise, and can be performed by two teams competing against each other. The boys of each team line up with their legs wide apart and each foot touching that of the boy next in line.

The boys on the ends of the line touch chalk marks to keep them in line, and on the chalk mark at one end is a small block of wood or other object that will not roll.

At the word " Go ! " the boy nearest the block of wood bends sideways, picks it up and passes it over his head to the next boy, who passes it on with a clean-cut movement, until the block reaches the end of the line. Here the last boy passes it over his head, transfers it to his other hand and places it on the chalk mark. This done, the block is passed back again to the original end in exactly the same way. Bear in mind that there must be no twisting or stooping when playing this game ; it is first and foremost an exercise !

Another side-bending exercise is the BACK TO BACK, BENDING SIDEWAYS movement. Standing in pairs the boys

[*Fox Photos.*

A DISPLAY BY SCHOOLBOYS.

have their feet astride and hook each other's elbows. Then they bend sideways to right and left. Next, the arms can be raised sideways in line with the shoulders and the hands clasped instead of the elbows being hooked.

EXERCISES FOR THE STOMACH

An excellent stomach-muscle exercise is to take up a position like a frog and jump along on hands and feet. This can be made into a race and will prove quite exciting. The familiar Wheelbarrow Race provides another good exercise for stomach muscles.

Raising the trunk off the floor with the legs and feet just touching makes another splendid abdominal exercise, and can be done several times every morning after you have performed the usual exercises of shooting the arms out sideways, upwards and then down again.

More good exercises consist of standing upright and raising each leg sideways ; of placing the hands on the hips and bending as far back as possible ; of placing the hands behind the head in a locked position and moving the head to the right and left ; lying face downward on the floor and raising the body by the hands, repeating the movement as many times as possible.

One thing to remember about physical exercises : to be beneficial they must be carried out regularly. It is of no use doing them just when you feel like it. Practise them morning and evening—all the year round—and watch your muscles develop.

[*Fox Photos.*

STRENUOUS EXERCISES THAT BENEFIT EVERY PART OF THE BODY.

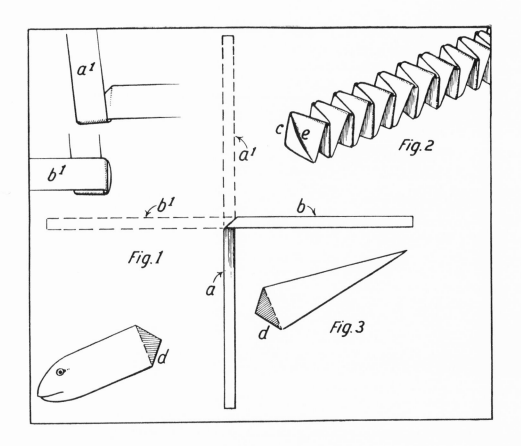

A PAPER SNAKE

TAKE a long narrow strip of paper, say about half an inch wide and 24 inches or more long. Fold this across at right angles at the middle, as shown in Figure 1. Then fold the length a over into the position a^1, shown in dotted lines, after which, fold over b into the dotted position b^1. Then fold a^1 down to its original position a, and fold b^1 back to its original position b. Fold a up into position a^1 again, and so on with alternate backward and forward folds until all the paper strip has been exhausted in the formation of a folded body which can be opened out concertina wise to produce the body of the snake, part of which is shown in Figure 2. The two free ends c are to be gummed together and tucked in so as to form a pocket as at e, before the body is pulled out.

173

The resemblance to a snake may be improved by adding a head and a tail piece such as are shown in Figure 3, the portions *d* being bent over, gummed and inserted into the pockets *e* at each end of the snake's body.

THE BOY IN THE BOTTLE

THE camera lends itself to many dodges and "fakes." Here is one. Photograph a boy against a plain dark background. The exposure should only be long enough to show the figure distinctly. Let the exact position of the boy's figure be marked on the ground glass of the focusing screen. Now on the same photographic plate take a photograph of an empty bottle, placed against the dark background, and focused so that the outline of the bottle shall enclose the outline of the boy, allowing twice as long an exposure as was given when taking the photograph of the boy. Develop, fix and print in the usual way.

Should all have gone well an extraordinary picture will be obtained of a boy cribbed, cabined and confined within the apparently impossible dimensions of a bottle.

There are, of course, innumerable adaptations of this simple "fake," and endless amusement may be afforded. In exactly the same manner a dog, cat or any other animal, may be photographed as confined in a glass jam jar, or you might try one of baby, or big brother Arthur in a milk-bottle !

THE OLD GATE.

OUT-OF-DOORS WITH A
SKETCH-BOOK

ONE of the most delightful outdoor hobbies for at least nine months in the year is sketching. The full equipment costs a few pence only, and there is no need to be a skilled artist before you can make a start.

Every artist has to begin at the bottom, there is no need to draw cubes, prisms and triangles, and Nature is the finest teacher of all.

To begin, let us consider our simple " kit." A real sketch-book can be bought for a shilling or so, or you can use a small-size pad of cream-laid notepaper, preferably white. If you intend keeping your work in pencil, a book with a " rough " surface is best, but smoother paper is necessary if you are going to ink in the sketches at home.

There are plenty of good pencils on the market, and as they are really very cheap, it pays to buy the best. Choose " B " for light work and outlines, " 4B " for general work, and " 6B " for rich, velvet shading. A nice, soft piece of india-rubber completes your whole equipment.

The question now arises : " What shall we draw ? " Well, nature provides subjects in such numbers that it is difficult to know where to begin, but you cannot do better than start with twigs and leaves. From these you learn how trees are constructed, how to draw foliage, and later on how to include everything in landscape.

You must, however, remember a very simple rule all through. No matter what you are drawing, *keep your work simple.* If you never forget this, you will find a tremendous number of difficulties are smoothed away as you progress. There is no need to draw

Cumulus clouds.

every vein in the leaf, every leaf on the tree, every brick or stone in a wall, and so on. That would be mere drudgery. If you look

A storm cloud.

at other people's work, and the examples given here, you will realise that a lot is left out altogether, and it is this secret which makes successful art.

Never put down a line unless you are certain it is necessary. "If in doubt, leave it out" is very important. Needless shading and useless lines only spoil good work, so from the start keep everything simple.

Now let us get down to real work. Look at that old gate, with the tree near it. It would make an excellent first study. First of all, half close your eyes, and you will see that a lot of detail is now missing. The trees bear leaves in *masses* of light and shade. The gate is shaded in two or perhaps three tones only, instead of every bit of grain being visible. That is what you have to draw—the simplest possible *mass* only.

With your "B" pencil, lightly sketch the

A timber fence.

176

Old buildings and brick-work.

gate, and never bear on the paper so that marks show through. Now continue with the wall in a similar manner, just drawing the outline only of the worn stones. Hold the sketch at arm's length and compare it with the original. Does it look right? Don't be discouraged if at first it is not just what you would like. One advantage of light pencil work is that it can so easily be erased.

When you have succeeded in making the outlines a little like the scene, take the " 4B " pencil, with not too sharp a point, and go over the outlines, taking care that you do not make them all alike or of the same thickness. Where there is shadow you can use a thicker or deeper line, but never use smeary shading by rubbing the pencil to and fro on the paper. Nice, even strokes of varying thickness look much better and not so " woolly."

Birch Trunk   Sycamore Trunk

Now, with the "6B," and again using clean strokes, fill in the deepest shadows, and you will probably be surprised to see how much like the actual scene your sketch looks. But don't forget that golden rule about simplicity, and leave out everything that is unnecessary. You will now be able to discover that three or at the most, four tones are all that is required to make good sketches—white paper, light outlines, medium shadow, and deep shading.

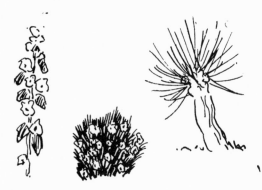

Leaves, twigs and foliage.

Rough sketches—hollyhock, flowers in grass and a pollarded willow.

Tree trunks are excellent models for the beginner, and if you have a little patience and study the outline and nature of the bark, you will soon have little difficulty in drawing it. Look at the examples here given and find out how the various strokes actually represent the type of tree. It's quite an easy matter after a little practice!

Twigs and leaves can be drawn either out-of-doors or at home, and the careful young artist will again study each type and find out how to depict the character of the subject.

Now in summer every tree has thousands of leaves, but no

Character in Trees and their Trunks.

Sycamore

Willow

Oak

sane person would dream of drawing every one of them ! Again half close your eyes and observe the masses. Lightly pencil in the main outline of the tree, follow this up with the lightest shade masses, and finally put in the deep patches which will give your tree " body " and depth. And notice that certain strokes of the pencil can actually depict the type of leaf on the tree, even at a distance.

Old walls, cottages, barns and ruins are fine subjects for the pencil. They have not the severe lines of modern buildings, and are much easier to draw. Here again a faint outline is followed by the lightest shadows and finally by the deep shades. Don't put in every stone or brick. A few dotted here and there will be enough to show the type of structure. Even the windows are best shown by omitting a lot of detail.

A few more efforts and you should be able to produce sketches

Fir

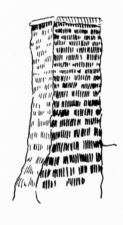

that will please not only yourself but your friends, and here are a few final hints :

Grass can be represented by a few simple strokes, tall or short. In landscape work, the foreground should be more detailed and in heavier line ; the middle distance lighter, and the far distance lightest of all. Skies can be drawn in a variety of ways and drawing clouds is great fun.

HOW TO WHISTLE A DOOR SHUT

OF course, you have all heard of doors being opened and closed by means of an invisible ray. But have you heard about one that will shut in reply to a whistle ? The response of solid bodies to sound vibration can be made use of in a very striking experiment of this nature. A little care is necessary in the construction of the apparatus, but the broad details are as follows. I have actually arranged similar apparatus to shut an ordinary door, but it is safer at first to try a small door in a model doll's house.

First of all make sure that your door moves very easily on well-oiled hinges, as you will have no energy to spare. Now down the side of the door stretch a banjo string between two strings, so that you can loosen or tighten it as required. A small fraction of an inch from the string place a terminal, so that when the wire is plucked it strikes the terminal. From this terminal a wire leads to a small electro-magnet like that used in electric door bells. A wire from one of the screws holding the banjo wire leads to a battery and then on to the other terminal of the electro-magnet. Thus you will see that your banjo wire is really a switch, and when vibrated, closes the circuit bringing the electro-magnet into action.

Screw the electro-magnet inside the box or house, so that it is a fraction of an inch from the inner edge of the door when open, and opposite fix a small iron " contact." If you now sound a whistle, the string will vibrate. If it fails to respond, try tightening it until it sounds much the same note as the whistle. The vibration of the string will close up the circuit and bring the electro-magnet into action so that the metal is attracted and the door closed. If there does not seem to be sufficient power in the electro-magnet, weight the bottom of the door, so that the slightest pull will close it.

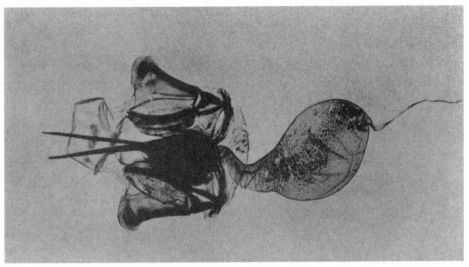

By courtesy of]

THE STING OF A BEE.

F. Davidson & Co.

UNDER THE MICROSCOPE

IT is impossible to indicate a thousandth part of the wonders that the microscope will show you ; living animals fighting battles in a speck of human blood ; the stings on the leaf of a nettle looking like the blades of bayonets ; a wonderful web of silver cells filled with moving fluid on a speck of a rose petal ; the coiled-up tongue of a butterfly as large as a clock spring ; a drop of water teeming with " animals " ; minute grains of sand that look like crystal boulders, and many others.

Let us imagine—and hope—that you are already the proud possessor of a microscope and of the necessary outfit for examining the tiny objects around us on every hand.

You have ready some water, a little glycerine, some glass slips and cover glasses, your micro-forceps and dissecting-knife.

It will not be necessary to go far for " specimens." There are possibly some flowers in a vase on the table, anyway, there are leaves in the garden, or somewhere close at hand. Take up a leaf and with your dissecting-knife make an incision into the leaf skin ; do not cut through, just pierce the outer skin, and then with your micro-forceps tear away a tiny piece of the epidermis (skin) and place it on your glass slip, pressing it in contact with the glass. Now place it on the stage of the microscope and focus it. Whatever the leaf may be, the sight of it under the microscope will fill you with amazement. You will find a veritable forest of hairs arranged in beautiful geometrical designs.

The arabis found in almost every garden will show you strangely-formed hairs standing up like leafless trees, with trunk and branches complete ; a piece of the leaf of the deutzia shows brilliant star-shaped hairs packed closely together ; a piece of nettle leaf will display wonderful jointed hairs with the deadly "stings" looking like formidable daggers.

From leaves we may proceed to twigs. From the smallest twig or stalk cut a thin slice and look at it under the microscope. The designs will be wonderful and startling.

Now look at some of the articles in the pantry ; a few grains of sugar show each crystal with a dis-

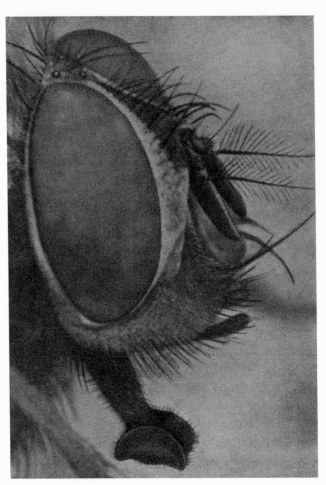

[*H. Bastin.*

SIDE FACE OF A BLUEBOTTLE FLY. (Greatly magnified.)
Note the curiously-shaped antennæ, the large compound eyes, and the three small " simple " eyes on the forehead.

tinctive shape and wonderful colour ; salt crystals, too, assume strange shapes, like the designs on your window after a sharp frost. Look also at a piece of sultana or raisin, a piece of rice (cut), a tiny piece of fat (suet or beef or mutton).

Pollen dust from flowers will prove most fascinating, the pollen grains of various flowers being all of different shape. You will find

The terrifying appearance of a house-spider, as seen by a doomed fly. Note the eight small eyes upon the top of the head and the huge pair of poison-injecting jaws.

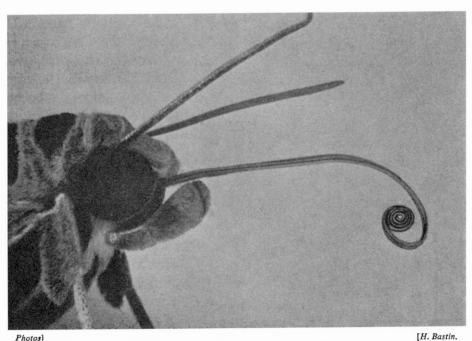

Photos]   *[H. Bastin.*

HEAD AND TONGUE OF A MOTH.
The tongue can be unrolled to penetrate the deepest recesses of flowers.

that the keen edge of a razor looks anything but sharp under the microscope, whilst the edge of a table knife looks like a huge snow-covered mountain.

The wings of insects are astonishing and very beautiful ; look at a fly's wing, a gnat's wing, a piece of a beetle's wing, and a ladybird's wing.

Some slides already prepared you will have to buy. The eye of a spider, the eye of a bee, the tongue of a butterfly, the leg of a spider, the teeth of a snail, are but a few of the very wonderful objects you should view under the microscope.

[James's Press.

The foot of a spider. (Greatly magnified.)

Our illustrations show some even more wonderful examples. Look at the sting of a bee, on page 239. It is a very formidable weapon when seen under the microscope.

Illustrations Bureau.

Head and antennæ of a Beetle. (Greatly magnified.)

The face of a Bluebottle Fly shown on page 240, under the microscope appears a fearsome object. The top illustration on this page clearly shows the wonderful combs at the tip of a spider's foot, while the lower illustration, showing the head and antennæ of a Beetle, is extremely weird. The illustrations on page 241, of the Head and Tongue of a Moth, and the Face of a Spider are extraordinary, to say the least of them.

THREE TRICKS WITH COINS

THE PENNIES BALANCE

FOR the first trick lay three pennies with thick edges edge to edge in a row in the left hand, and upon them place a thin strip of wood, slightly longer than the three pennies placed on end. This should have been concealed in the palm of the right hand. Grip the ends of the stick between the thumb and second finger of the right hand, at the same time holding the top and bottom coins tightly. The coins can then be raised perpendicularly, and shown as if self-supported upon their own edges.

THE METALLIC SPHERE

For the second trick place a half-crown flat on the table, then seize it between two pins held at the extremities of the same diameter. The coin may then be raised without trouble. Blow against the upper surface, and the coin will revolve with tremendous speed, and appear like a metallic sphere.

THE MAGIC PENNY

In the third trick gum the rim of a small tumbler, and spread a piece of white paper across it. Then cut away the edges, so that the top of the tumbler resembles a drum. The tumbler is then laid rim downwards upon a sheet of white paper.

A penny is laid upon the paper, and the performer places a paper cylinder (which is exhibited to show that it is empty) over the glass, and the two are lifted and placed (still top downwards) over the penny.

The cylinder is then removed, and of course the penny, being hidden by the paper drum stretched over the bottom or hollow end of the glass, appears to have vanished.

Care should be taken always to place the cover over the glass, when passing it over or away from the coin, also to keep the glass always on the sheet of white paper, otherwise the pasted end will be exposed.

HANDKERCHIEF TRICKS

TAKE a piece of stout wire, about twenty inches in length and with a very small hook or point on one end, and push it up the left sleeve, leaving the hook towards the hand. Take a handkerchief by the corners diagonally, twist it in the form of a rope, then attempt to balance it on a finger of the left hand. In this you will be unsuccessful, and the handkerchief will collapse.

Now take a corner of the handkerchief in the right hand, and hook it to the wire protruding from your sleeve ; drag this through your left hand so that the wire is hidden by the handkerchief. Directly the whole of the wire has been pulled out of the sleeve, again twist the handkerchief ropewise—with the wire inside. You can then quite easily balance the handkerchief on your finger. The hooked end, of course, must be at the top, to prevent the handkerchief from slipping down.

Roll two silk handkerchiefs ropewise, and let anyone tie them together and while pretending that you have a very difficult knot to cope with, and that you doubt if you can manage to undo it, pull the knot about, until one handkerchief runs through the knot in practically a straight line. Mask what has been done as far as possible, and then show that the knot has not been untied, but do not let it be examined. Hold it in one hand, and cover with another handkerchief, or else with one hand behind the back.

The other part of the knot can then be easily pushed off the straight piece with two fingers only.

Let someone tie your wrists together with a handkerchief, not too tightly, and then let them place a long piece of stout cord between the arms and round (i.e. over and under) the handkerchief. Get an assistant to hold both ends of the cord, and immediately he has secured them, thrust the hands forward, bend the fingers of the right hand down, pull the cord up between the handkerchief, pass the back of the hand underneath the loop, and tell the person who is holding the cord to pull it hard. The rope goes off the back of the hand, underneath the handkerchief, which it does not displace.

THE BREAST STROKE.

BE A BETTER SWIMMER

MANY swimmers have a slovenly style in the water through bad teaching or because they have " picked up " the art without proper knowledge. This article, though written for beginners, should nevertheless be studied by all swimmers ; the better ones checking up on their strokes to make certain that they are not handicapping themselves by bad movements.

For the breast stroke, the oldest method of swimming known to man, you must learn the movements of the legs and of the arms separately before attempting to do them together. You must not bend the knees upwards only, as is done in walking, but force them to right and left. The heels must be slightly separated and turned towards each other.

The backward " kick " of the legs is most important and gives the stroke its real power. Watch a frog or a toad just before it makes its leap, and you will see the perfect leg action for a breast-stroke swimmer. The thrust with the legs should be made at the exact moment when the arms are fully stretched forward.

Learn to make your strokes without effort ; glide rather than " work " your way through the water. Keep perfectly calm ; do not become scared if your head happens to go under the water. Bear in mind that the essential movement of the arms when doing the breast-stroke consists of bringing the rigidly stretched arms back, just as if you were pushing the water away from you. Put genuine power into those arm movements, and, if your legs are doing their work, you will feel your body ploughing through the water.

Even after you have learned to keep yourself afloat and are actually making progress through the water, practise that leg "kick" as often as you can, by holding on to the rail at the swimming baths and thrusting out with the legs.

"Early confidence" practice.

THE SIDE-STROKE

In this stroke the two arms do not move at the same time, but work one after the other ; you use one arm and both legs together. As with all forms of true swimming, the power comes from the legs and not from the arms. The latter push the water away, and the

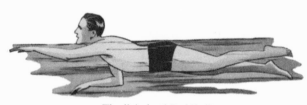

The "Animal Paddle."

former propel the body into the vacant space, as it were.

When you are learning the side-stroke it is a good plan to start with a few breast-strokes first, and then, as the arms return, turn slightly over on the side and begin the side-stroke. This means that the leg that is uppermost will take up the perfectly natural position of being bent across the lower one. It is also a good idea to learn the side-stroke on both sides. Not only will this give you confidence; it is also restful.

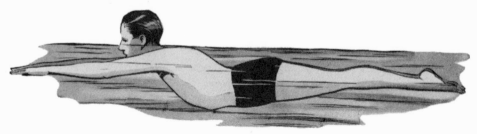

The Breast Stroke—shoot the arms out straight in front.

FLOATING

Everyone can learn to float success-
fully, particularly in salt water. When
floating, all the muscles must be
relaxed and the lungs filled with air.
The chest must not be held rigid.
Breath is inhaled through the nostrils
and *not* the mouth.

In order to prevent the legs, which
are heavy with muscles, from sinking,
fling the arms at full length above
the head, with only the hands and
wrists out of water, palms upwards
and cupped.

Learn to float face downwards as
well as upwards. This is useful for

Diving.

" plunging " or skimming through the water just underneath the
surface. When floating face downwards, you should keep the
muscles rigid.

DIVING

The important point to remember when diving is to *spring
upwards and outwards* with the arms, body and legs in a straight
line. Do not merely fall forward with the head and shoulders bent.
If you do, you will probably sting your skin and " plop " when you
enter the water.

Always enter the water with the palms apart, not touching each
other.

The spring-board at the deep end of the baths is the best place
for taking-off. Stand with the toes just over the edge and heels
touching, the head and
shoulders erect and the
arms straight at the sides.
As you spring upwards,
shoot the arms above
the head, keep the palms
outward, fore-fingers
touching, and tuck your
head between the arms
as you enter the water.

The Crawl. The favourite racing stroke.

The Crawl, showing how the arms and legs are worked.

Do not attempt fancy dives, such as the " swallow," the " jack-knife " and others, until you have mastered the art of entering the water cleanly and with a minimum of splash. Most of all, remember to spring UPWARDS and OUTWARDS. In that lies the whole secret of successful diving.

GENERAL HINTS FOR SWIMMERS

Do not go too far out when swimming at places you do not know. Indeed, it is stupid to venture far in any circumstances if you are alone.

Do not stay in too long. Come out and have a brisk rub down with a rough towel the moment you begin to feel cold. Even famous swimmers do this unless they are engaged on an important long-distance swim.

Once you have learnt to swim, gain confidence by swimming dog-fashion, paddling along on the back, treading-water, doing surface dives and generally convincing yourself that you are perfectly

The Back Crawl, showing the action of arms and legs.

A HEADLONG DIVE.

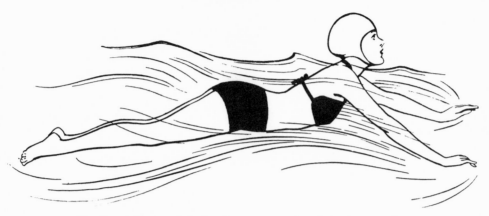

The Breast Stroke ; bringing the arms round and the legs together.

at home in the water. Face breakers and grow used to being slapped in the face.

Practise breathing deeply, so that you will not have to keep coming up for air when doing the Crawl or other stroke necessitating burying the face in the water. Good breathing and breath-holding mean a great deal in swimming and diving.

Do not " trickle " into the water. Plunge in bravely and fearlessly, even if you have not yet learned to swim. In the latter case, however, do not do so at the deep end of the baths. On the other hand, be very careful not to dive into water that is too shallow, risking striking your head on the bottom of the bath.

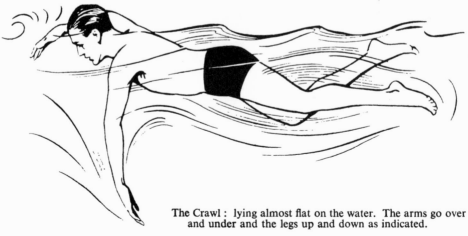

The Crawl : lying almost flat on the water. The arms go over and under and the legs up and down as indicated.

ON A ROOF-TOP PLAYGROUND.

[*Fox Photos.*

ROUND GAMES ARE GREAT FUN

THERE are so many good round games that it is difficult to pick out the best. Here, however, are a number of old and new ones that can be played by boys or girls either out-of-doors or in a room or hall.

THREE LIVES

The players are arranged in a circle and each has three " lives." A " life " is lost every time he or she drops the ball thrown from hand to hand round the circle. Directly a player has lost all three " lives," he or she drops out of the game. The last one left in is the winner.

UP AND DOWN

The players are arranged in a ring and a ball is thrown from hand to hand as in the first game. But directly a player drops the ball, he or she must use only the right hand with which to catch.

The second time the ball is dropped, the player uses only the left hand. The third time the player goes on to one knee ; the fourth time, he or she drops to both knees, and finally is obliged to lie down. When on the knees or lying down, a player can use both hands, and if he manages to catch a ball in such an attitude he can go back to the previous position.

Should a player drop the ball when lying down, he or she is out of the game.

STATUES

In this game the ball is thrown to any one of the players, who are not necessarily round a circle. Directly a player drops the ball, he must stand in the position assumed when trying to catch it. He remains in this position until another player drops the ball, when he or she is released and can stand in a normal manner. This is great fun because of the strange attitudes taken up by those who miss the ball and must act as statues. The game should be played quickly.

TWIRLING THE PLATE

Here is a very simple yet exciting game. The leader gives each boy and girl a number when the players have been arranged in a circle. The leader then starts a plate spinning on the ground in the middle of the circle and, as the plate begins to slow down, calls out a number. Instantly the owner of the number must rush forward and grasp the plate, giving it another twirl before it sinks to the ground.

It is then the turn of this player to call out a number, and the game goes on until someone allows the plate to stop spinning. After this comes the fun of making that unlucky individual pay a forfeit, which can consist of crawling up the garden on all-fours ; walking along a row of flower-pots ; jumping a flower bed ; wheeling a very small doll's pram loaded with a glass of water ; hopping with one foot held ; lying down and getting up again with arms folded ; running backwards in a straight line, or lapping up a saucer of water !

BOUNCING BALL

The players are arranged in a circle—about two yards between each—and a ball is thrown into the centre. The nearest player rushes out and bounces the ball on its rebound, hitting it with the palm of the hand once and once only. The next player does the same and so on right round the circle. Any player bouncing the ball twice instead of once is out of the game, which goes on until there remains only one player, who is the winner. This is not so easy as it would seem.

THE DANGER ZONE

Here is a good game played with a newspaper. A sheet is placed in the centre of a circle formed by players holding hands. On the

[Fox Photos.

LEAP-FROG.

word " Go ! " the boys or girls have to bump against each other and endeavour to push each other on the paper. If a player so much as touches the paper he is " out."

The ring is then reformed without him and the game continues. The last player in, is, as usual, the winner. Do not forget that players must not loosen their hold on each other's hands. They must push only with their bodies. No kicking or treading on toes is allowed. Boys and girls should not be mixed for this game, as boys have greater strength than girls, and therefore are usually at an advantage.

GIANTS AND DWARFS

This is a very funny game and can be played in a circle or like

ROUND GAMES

Follow-my-Leader. The players march round in single file, then on the order " Giants " from the referee, they must march on tip-toe.

On the command " Dwarfs " they assume an almost sitting position and shuffle along as best they can until receiving the third order " Steady," when they march in a normal manner until another order is given of " Giants " or " Dwarfs."

The referee should not give " Giants " and " Dwarfs " regularly one after the other, but vary his orders by saying " Giants " or " Dwarfs " twice or even three times in succession. Should a player make a wrong move, he or she must leave the circle when ordered to do so by the referee.

HUNT THE RING

This is an indoor game, which can also be played out-of-doors, particularly when waiting for the kettle to boil at a picnic.

A long length of string is passed through a ring and joined to form a circle. The players also form a circle and take the string in their hands.

At the word " Go ! " they run the string through their hands, thus changing the position of the ring.

One player stands in the centre of the circle and, at intervals, may touch any hand he or she chooses. Directly that hand is touched it must be lifted and, should the ring be concealed beneath, the player caught out must go into the centre of the circle while the other player takes his or her place.

This game is very exciting if the player in the centre pretends to touch one hand and then rapidly darts away and touches another one.

ROUND THE WORLD

The boys and girls are all seated in a circle except one, who is blindfolded and placed in the centre. Each player has previously been given the name of a town or city to remember, and, should the player in the centre call out " London to New York," the two who represent " London " and " New York " must rush forward and change places while the blindfolded player tries to catch one of them. If he is successful, the captured player goes into the centre and proceeds to call out some other journey such as : " Paris to Bradford " or " Edinburgh to Belfast." If places for which there are no players are called, there is, of course, no movement.

ROUND GAMES

When played indoors, the boys and girls should sit on the floor or chairs.

TWOS AND THREES

This is a grand game that can be played by quite a large number of people. When one player has been chosen as "He," the others arrange themselves in a wide circle in pairs, one in front of the other. In one single group, however, there are *three*, and the last man in that group begins to run. This is the cue for "He" to try to catch him before he can slip into the circle and stand in front of another pair.

The moment he succeeds in doing this, the last man in that group must run and take his chance of being caught. The whole idea of the game is to make certain that there are never more than two people in a group.

In the event of "He" catching his prey before the latter can save himself by joining a new group, "He" changes places and at once runs in front of a group.

[*Fox Photos.*

MAKING RINGS ROUND THE LIFEBUOY—A ROUND GAME IN THE WATER
THAT REQUIRES CONSIDERABLE SKILL.

AN ATHLETIC DISPLAY. [Fox Photos.

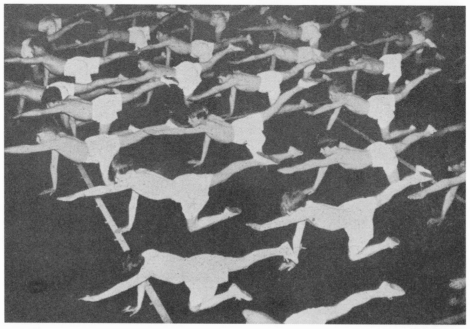

LEG AND ARM BALANCE. [Fox Photos.

SOME MORE GOOD TRICKS

THE MAGIC SIXPENCE

HERE is a good trick. Break a match in the middle so that it does not quite come in two, place the angle over the mouth of a bottle, and lay a sixpence on top. The problem is to drop the sixpence into the bottle without touching it. The solution is easy. Just let a drop of water fall from your finger on to the bend in the match. The wood will expand with the water, the angle will open, and the sixpence will drop into the bottle.

PENNY AND HALFPENNY TRICK

Another good " catch " is to lay a halfpenny on a piece of paper, draw its outline, and cut it out. Now lay a penny over the aperture and challenge anyone to pass the penny through the hole made by the halfpenny. Probably the majority of those present will declare that it is impossible, but you, knowing something of curved space, will promptly crumple the paper, so that it is bent about the hole, when the penny can be gently coaxed through from underneath.

EATING CANDLES

Candles that you can eat are easily prepared. Out of bananas, or apples, cut and shape some mock candle ends, making them as much as possible like candles that have been burnt down. Fashion some slips of sweet almonds to resemble wicks and stick them into the mock candles, light for an instant, so as to make their tops black, blow them out again, and they are ready for use. Place in candle sticks, and light when performing.

The almond will flame for a few moments, put the candles into your mouth, and chew and swallow.

THE MAGIC WRITING

Here is another good trick. Sharpen a piece of French chalk to a point, and with it write on an ordinary looking-glass. Polish lightly with a silk handkerchief, and the writing will disappear. Hand the glass to a member of the audience, and request him or her to breathe upon it, and the writing will reappear. Polish the glass again carefully, and the experiment can be repeated.

SOME MORE GOOD TRICKS

WINE AND WATER TRICK

Dip two wine glasses of the same size into a basin of water, and before taking them out, place the brims together, so that they may be withdrawn full, one being inverted on the top or over the other. Then move them very slightly, so that a very small space may intervene between the rims. Take a third glass and drip from it some wine in such a manner that it spreads slowly over the foot of the inverted glass. When the wine has trickled down to the rims of the glasses, the ruddy drops will filter into them and ascend into the upper glass, thus demonstrating the difference in the densities of wine and water. Try this first over a sink or large basin.

THE MAGIC PAPER LOOPS

An interesting trick may be staged with three strips of paper, each two or three feet in length by one inch in width, paste, and a pair of scissors. Paste the ends of the first strip of paper together. Twist the second strip of paper once, and paste the ends of that together. Twist the third strip of paper twice, and paste the ends of that together also ; i.e. make three paper loops. Exhibit the first loop, and remark that the obvious effect if you cut it in half, strip-wise, will be to make two loops. The loops should then be cut. Now pick up the second loop and remark that you are going to do the same with this loop. Cut the loop of paper, and a loop twice the size will be produced. Now pick up the third loop, and cut that in the same manner, and two loops, one inside the other, will be produced. In the case of the loop with the double twist, it will require a little dexterity to keep this twist masked, especially when cutting the twist. The loops are, of course, prepared before the spectators enter the room.

THE MAGIC PEA

For this trick lay three walnut shells upon a table that has been covered with a cloth. A small ball or pea made of india-rubber is placed under the centre one, and the other two are shown not to be covering anything. Ask which shell the pea shall appear under, and, being told, push forward the other empty shell along the table about three inches with the first and second fingers. Do the same with the one that is covering the pea, and as it is moved forward, the pea will come out behind it as a natural effect. As it comes from under the shell cover it with the first and second fingers which are held together, then move the third shell forward with these two fingers, and in doing so place the pea underneath it. This is not at all a difficult trick to perform, very little practice being required, and although the onlookers may be very close, they will rarely see how it is done.

SMOKE RINGS

You may have seen someone smoking a pipe or cigarette who is able, after inhaling the smoke, to send it back in the form of beautiful rings into the air. In a still atmosphere these rings will remain quite perfect and float about for some while. It is really quite easy to make a box with which you can produce smoke rings as fast as you wish. Get a well-made card or wooden box which is rather longer than it is wide. One end of the box should be removed altogether and across this stretch a piece of cloth, fixing it with gum or glue. At the opposite end cut a round hole about an inch across. You are now ready to start making smoke rings. Get a piece of thick brown paper, light this for a moment and then blow out. The paper, which will now be smouldering and giving out a lot of smoke, is pushed in through the hole at the end of the box. Of course, in a moment the box is filled with smoke. All you have to do now is to give the cloth at the other end of the box a series of smart little taps. With every tap there will issue from the hole a perfect smoke ring, and you can send these out as fast as you like, one after the other. Sometimes one ring will overtake another and you get a very pretty effect. The smoke rings will continue to come out as long as there is any smoke left in the box.

THE SNAKE

You can make an amusing " snake " by drawing a spiral upon a piece of paper about three and a half inches in diameter, the lines being a quarter of an inch apart. If you cut round the spiral and put a pin through the top, the whole will rotate when held over a flame or draught.

THE DISAPPEARING CORK

By the aid of a round cork and a long hair an apparently miraculous sleight of hand trick can be made. If this hair is attached to the cork by pushing in the ends with a match, leaving a loop about two inches long, the hair can be slipped over the middle finger and the cork made to vanish by being dropped behind the outstretched hand.

THE PENCIL HAT PEG

Here is a very effective trick on entering a room. The performer, with hand covered by his hat, rubs a polished pencil, sharpened towards the side instead of in the usual way, sharply down the side of the door. The pencil will adhere to it, and a hat with a flat brim can be hung upon the pencil.

THE TWO GLASSES

When two glasses are placed one within the other, the inner glass can be removed by blowing into the gap. This is a good demonstration of the power of a rapidly moving stream of air.

TRICKS WITH EGGS

The Egg in the Bottle. Egg-shells owe their hardness to the presence of lime. If an egg is well soaked in strong vinegar for a few hours the lime is dissolved, and the shell will be so supple that the entire egg can be pressed through the neck of a narrow-necked bottle. If the bottle is then filled with water, the egg will regain its shape and the shell its hardness ; while the boy who has carefully carried out the experiment will have a busy time answering friends who want to know just how it was done.

Engraving on Eggs. We have seen that egg-shells contain lime which can be dissolved by strong vinegar. If, therefore, we draw or write on an egg-shell with a stick dipped in hot wax or tallow, as much of the shell as is protected by the wax will be unaffected if we place the egg in some strong vinegar. Leave it there for an hour or so and then remove the wax with some turpentine, when it will be found that the unprotected parts of the shell have been eaten away, leaving the writing in relief.

The Redwing.

OUT-OF-DOORS—IV

WHAT TO LOOK FOR IN WINTER

WINTER is not the dead season we may suppose, and on our walks there is a lot to see that we missed in the other seasons. For instance, we can now find lots of nests we missed when the leaves were on the trees, and if we examine some of the blackbirds' and thrushes' nests in the hedgerows, we shall find them full of dead leaves, berries, and nutshells, proving that they have become the homes of the wild mice.

Examining the tree trunks we shall find, wedged firmly in the cracks, empty nutshells, telling us that the beautiful slate-grey and orange nuthatch has been there.

Under the fir trees the cones will be found picked apart. If they are stripped to the stem, it is the work of the squirrel, but if the parts containing the seeds have been neatly split open, then we may be sure that crossbills have been there, and it is worth while keeping a watch for these strange birds.

Also, in the fir trees, and quite often in our gardens, Europe's

The Field Mouse.

tiniest bird will be seen—the gold-crest, only three and a half inches from tip of beak to tail. It has a lemon and orange-coloured streak on top of the head, and if we keep quite still, it will go on hunting quite close to us.

When all the summer visitors have departed in the movement south, other birds take their places and migrants from Scandinavia arrive. You may have been mysti-fied on dark nights by hearing a cry of " seep " repeated at intervals. This is the migrating cry of the redwing, a bird of the thrush family, which can be identified by its reddish flanks. Another bird of the thrush family to come is the fieldfare, larger than the redwing, and keeping in larger flocks. Its general grey colour and the call of " chack-chack-chack " will make you quite sure of having seen them.

Large numbers of birds now collect on the mud flats and in the tidal estuaries of our coasts, and if you are lucky enough to live near them, a visit will be well repaid. Redshank, green-shank, whimbrel, curlew, green and golden plover and a host of others will be seen, besides enormous flocks of wild duck and geese.

Dormice, field mice, voles and

The Grey Squirrel.

GOLDCRESTS.
These are Europe's tiniest birds, and can be identified by the lemon and orange-coloured streak on top of the head.

shrews are now busy gorging themselves with nuts, berries and other roadside delicacies. In this manner they obtain the necessary fat which enables them to live through the winter without venturing forth unless the weather is very mild. We may often disturb them at their feast, but on hearing the slightest strange noise, they vanish.

The nuthatch at its nest.

Few flowers bloom in winter, but there is always one or more to discover. That common weed, the shepherd's purse, will be found flowering at all times, and when you know that this despised plant is boiled and eaten as a vegetable in China, it becomes quite interesting ! On the birch trees the catkins are easy to see. They were formed in the autumn, but will not be ripe for another two months.

A few bats will be seen on the wing during winter if the weather is mild, and the commonest kind, the pipistrelle, is often out after early insects at dusk. The bat is the only animal that can actually fly, *yet it has no wings*, for the flying apparatus is merely the membrane between the toes of its front feet ! Although some kinds, like the long-eared, are quite large and look fierce at close quarters, they are perfectly harmless to human beings, and feed only on moths and beetles caught on the wing.

WHAT TO LOOK FOR IN WINTER

Shepherd's purse.

If you look carefully at dead bracken stems lying on the ground, you will probably discover a very interesting growth, the bird's nest fungus. It is very small, but at close quarters looks just like a tiny bird's nest complete with eggs !

Even the bare trees of winter are full of interest, for the buds are forming, having pushed last summer's leaves from the stems, and we can easily tell each kind of tree from its twigs and buds.

Although most of us are in the habit of recognising trees by their leaves, flowers or fruits, winter is the time to get to know them more intimately, for then, when their branches are bare, we must study their contour, their method of branching and their resting buds—every kind of tree has its own characteristics, and the little resting buds, if you study them, almost invariably reveal the identity of the tree. The oak is easy to spot once you have carefully examined its little blunt, irregular buds and compared them with others. Elm buds, too, are quite distinctive, sharp-pointed little things set on very distinctive brackets in a spiral on the twigs. These are the leaf buds ; the quite round flower buds will possibly be found on the same twig. Perhaps the most elegant of all buds on

Birds'-nest fungus.

British trees are the long and slim buds of the beech. The egg-shaped buds of the sycamore are equally distinctive and are easy to recognise. The biggest and most important looking of buds, bed-post knob type at the ends of twigs, and glistening with varnish, are those of

A bat.

the horse chestnut. All have their distinguishing characteristics and are worthy of study and comparison when opportunity occurs.

Altogether Winter is a good season for walks, and there is always something to discover.

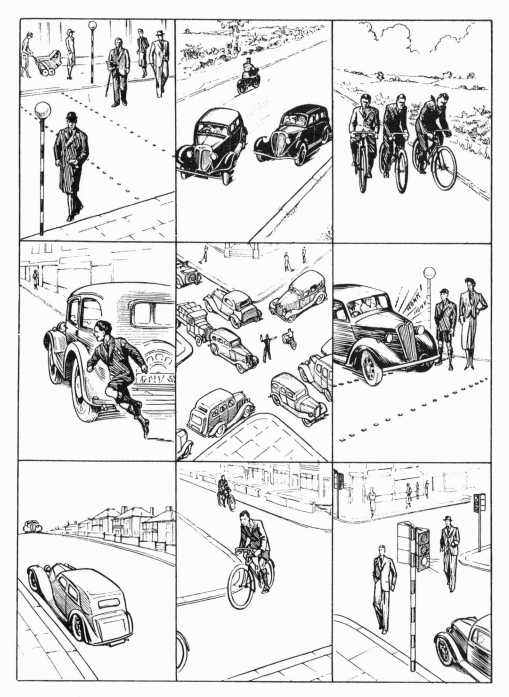

WHAT IS WRONG HERE?

In each of the above nine illustrations there is something that is obviously wrong.
Can you spot it at a glance?   For answers see next page.

WHAT IS WRONG HERE?

Solutions to Pictures on page 211.

1. Beacons are on wrong side of crossing and pedestrians are crossing diagonally instead of straight over.

2. Motor car " cutting in "—a most dangerous practice.

3. Cyclists riding three abreast.

4. Running out behind a stationary car.

5. Cars on wrong side and policeman round the wrong way.

6. Pedestrians should cross and car stop.

7. Standing car should face down hill and wheels be turned in.

8. Cyclist cutting corner on wrong side.

9. Pedestrians crossing when green traffic light is on.

THE EXPANDING POSTCARD

THIS may be presented as a magical trick, the performer offering to do the apparently impossible feat of passing himself through a postcard. The challenge having been accepted, the postcard is cut with a knife or scissors as shown in Figure 1.

First a longitudinal cut *a-a* is made, stopping short of the end of the card. Then two series of cuts *b* are made inwards from the two longitudinal outer edges, stopping just short of the cut *a-a*. Thirdly, two series of cuts *c* are made outwardly from the centre cut *a-a*, in the spaces between the cuts *b*, but not extending quite to the outer edges of the card.

When the cutting is completed, the card is pulled out by the ends A, as shown in Figure 2, until it can be passed over the head, and eventually over the body. Success or non-success in passing the card over the body depends upon the closeness together of the cuts *b* and *c*. The closer they are together the greater will be the expanded length of the card.

Instead of a postcard, other unlikely articles may be used for this trick, such, for example, as laurel or other large leaves.

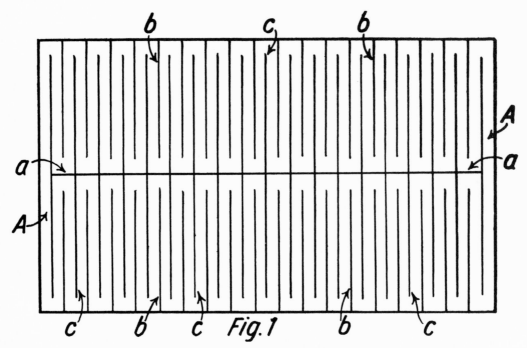

Fig. 1

The card cut as described on page 212.

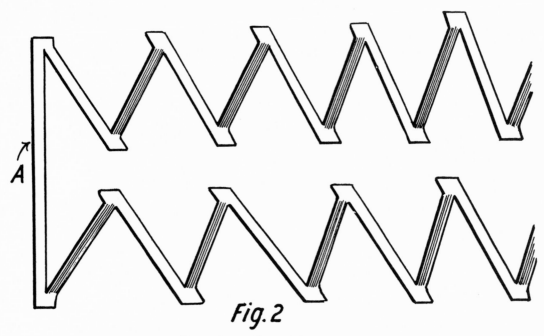

Fig. 2

The card expanding as it is drawn out.

SOME MORE INDOOR GAMES
WITH PAPER AND PENCIL

A BASKET OF FLOWERS

Every solution is the name of a well-known flower.

Solutions

1. A household implement — Broom
2. A tree, and part of a pig — Hollyhock
3. A bird, and a bad word — Crocus
4. A well-dressed wild beast — Dandelion
5. An article of food, and a vessel — Buttercup
6. A game, and a fabulous animal — Snapdragon
7. Crystallised sugar, and a bunch of grass — Candytuft
8. An animal, and an article of wearing apparel — Foxglove
9. An animal, and a petticoat — Cowslip
10. A man's name, and an old-fashioned piece of office equipment — Jonquil
11. A vehicle, and the people of England — Carnation
12. A pebble, and part of a whip — Stonecrop
13. A colour, and a musical instrument — Bluebell
14. Frugality — Thrift
15. Worn in winter — Furze
16. Male member of a family, and part of a plant — Sunflower
17. Something white, and a globule of moisture — Snowdrop
18. Earth, and to give in exchange for money — Groundsel

SOME BIRDS

The answers suggested by the statements are the names of birds.

Solutions

1. An action performed in eating — Swallow
2. Portion of a whole; and a range of hills — Partridge
3. A famous English architect — Wren
4. Equality, and a state of decay — Parrot
5. To dodge the head — Duck
6. Slang term expressing boastfulness — Crow

SOME MORE INDOOR GAMES WITH PAPER AND PENCIL

		Solutions
7.	A monarch, and a toiler of the sea	Kingfisher
8.	Cockney term for a certain animal ; to perform an act of devotion	Osprey
9.	To sell goods	Hawk
10.	Something bright, and a moorland plant	Starling
11.	A vegetable, and the name of a male bird	Peacock
12.	A schoolboy frolic	Lark
13.	The name of a disease	Thrush
14.	Abbreviated periodical, and a popular dish	Magpie

TURNING THE TABLE

The solutions are all words ending with " table."

		Solutions
1.	A table that will suit any purpose	Adaptable
2.	A table you can sell	Marketable
3.	A table for the lazy man	Comfortable
4.	A table that will bring good results	Profitable
5.	A table that will not be useful	Unsuitable
6.	A table a burglar can take away	Portable
7.	A table that will not be left behind	Unforgettable
8.	A table you must not doubt	Indubitable
9.	A table you cannot avoid	Inevitable
10.	A table that is not very smart	Disreputable
11.	A table that is pleasant to the taste	Palatable
12.	A table that is known for good conduct	Respectable
13.	A table you cannot improve upon	Unbeatable
14.	A table of importance	Notable
15.	A table that does your bidding	Tractable
16.	A table that is boundless	Illimitable.
17.	A table you cannot copy	Inimitable
18.	A table that is good to eat	Vegetable
19.	A very delightful table	Delectable
20.	A table easily annoyed	Irritable

SOME MORE INDOOR GAMES WITH PAPER AND PENCIL

KATE

The word which is suggested by each of the sentences given below ends with the syllable -*cate*.

		Solutions
1.	She often wrote home from school	Communicate
2.	Sometimes her letters were imaginative	Fabricate
3.	She avoided answering her parents' questions	Prevaricate
4.	And tried to bolster up her doubtful statements	Vindicate
5.	Schooldays ended and her desk was left empty	Vacate
6.	Her mother taught her housekeeping	Domesticate
7.	She lost her youthful simplicity	Sophisticate
8.	Her fiancé was a barrister	Advocate
9.	He heartily returned her affection	Reciprocate
10.	They got a certain document from the registrar	Certificate
11.	Their wedding presents included two similar gifts from different friends	Duplicate
12.	The church was crowded and the atmosphere was extremely close	Suffocate
13.	At the breakfast one visitor took too much wine	Intoxicate
14.	Grandfather was very slow and thorough in eating	Masticate
15.	The bride's father prophesied that the pair would be happy	Prognosticate
16.	For their honeymoon they went to a quiet village	Rusticate

THE TIRESOME LETTER

Players are asked to write down a list of objects on the left-hand side of their slips of paper. The list can be compiled by the company, if you like, each taking a turn to name an object. Then decide upon a letter of the alphabet—by a dip into a book at, say, " Page 12, line 4, and the 5th letter," or use any letter the players may suggest. Now the game begins. The letter selected has to be used as the initial for every one of the objects in the list.

Here is a suitable list : Flower, country, trade, drink, author, song, motto, vehicle, girl's name, novel, fruit, street name, advertisement, bird, animal, town, tree, mineral or precious stone, article of furniture.

If the letter decided upon is " R," one player might write : " Rose, Roumania, riveting," and so on. The object is to aim at uncommon words. This is the method of scoring. Suppose there are ten players. If a player has a word that no one else has thought of, he scores 10 ; if two have thought of the word they each score 9 ; and so on.

BOOK TITLES

Player No. 1 thinks of the title of a book (it should be fairly well-known) and it is the object of the others to guess it by finding out what letters it contains. Let us suppose Player No. 1 decides upon *David Copperfield*. He writes this on his paper and numbers the letters thus :—

D	A	V	I	D		C	O	P	P	E	R	F	I	E	L	D
1	2	3	4	5		6	7	8	9	10	11	12	13	14	15	16

Then he announces that his chosen title contains 16 letters. The players write numbers 1 to 16 on their papers in readiness for filling in the letters.

Those present now take it in turns to question No. 1. His neighbour says, " Are there any E's in it ? " The answer is, " Yes, numbers 10 and 14," whereupon all the players insert those two E's above their appropriate numbers. The next says, " Are there any B's ? " " No ! " says No. 1, and scores a mark for himself. This will go on until someone guesses what the title is ; it will probably become apparent before the letters are completely filled in. Every time a letter that is not in the chosen title is suggested, No. 1 will score a mark.

When the title is guessed, No. 2 will take a turn, and so on round the circle, the winner being the one who has scored most points by selecting a difficult title.

NOISES OFF

Players are provided with pencils and papers. They maintain absolute silence, while from behind a curtain or screen a number of different sounds are made. The players have to write down their guesses. Here are suggestions for sounds that can be made :

1.	Pouring water	7.	Winding a clock
2.	Cleaning knives	8.	Striking a match
3.	Bouncing a ball	9.	Opening a newspaper
4.	Dropping a pin	10.	Gargling
5.	Tearing linen	11.	Sharpening a pencil
6.	Bursting a paper bag	12.	Scratching a balloon.

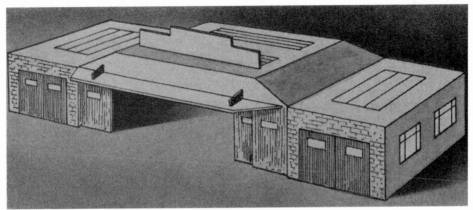

A MODEL GARAGE.

HOW TO MAKE A MODEL MOTOR GARAGE

THIS garage is quite simple to make as most of the difficult constructional work is avoided by the use of two strong cardboard boxes. These boxes are used for the ends and take all the weight of the roof and shelter.

Various strong boxes can be had from the grocers. For my model I used two " Stork " margarine boxes. These are 9 inches by 7 inches by 6 inches high. They should be opened out flat so that the windows can be put in while in the flat stage. Wide flaps will be found in the two short ends and these should be reduced to 1 inch in width. Take out the doors in the front short end, making these 4½ inches wide by 5 inches high. Provide small windows in the doors about 1 inch high and 1½ inches long. On the long side, which must face out from the garage, allow two windows 2 inches from the ground and 1½ inches high by 2 inches wide. There will be no need to put windows in the end, or in the other side. In the bottom of the box, which becomes the roof later, cut out a panel 4 inches by 6 inches. This serves as a fanlight and allows light into the box, which would otherwise be dark. Carry all these instructions out for the box to be placed on the opposite side. All windows can now be covered in with cellophane, or the waxed paper found in the packets of biscuits sold by bakers or grocers could be used. Such paper is ideal because one can paint in black strokes with a small brush and black enamel. The tops of the boxes can be

215

The back of the motor garage.

painted with grey paint. For the width of one inch up from the
bottom should be used the tiny red-brick paper which can be had
from most " Hobbies " shops. Do not, under any circumstances,
use the large red-brick paper. The area above this should be covered
with slate-grey tile paper. The surrounds of the windows should be
lined in with black enamel. Cover the doors with wood-grained
paper or paint with Poster colours.

The rear section is made up from a strong cardboard lid. I have
found that drapers have some good boxes for this purpose. The
width of your garage can be governed by the size of this piece.
I have made a garage of this type to hold twelve fair-sized motors
quite well. This section is just left in its flat stage with a wide flap
for strength along the bottom. The two ends are cut to slope as
they will later take the roof. Windows can be cut now and should be
about 1 inch from the base, 2 inches wide and about $2\frac{1}{2}$ inches high.
The centre ones should be taller in proportion to the height of your
cardboard. Lines for window bars can be marked in after the
windows have been filled in with the waxed paper. The covering for
this should be red brick and slate tile paper as used on the two boxes.

The front support for the roof forms the shelter and also the
slide for the doors. If your garage is fairly wide, you will have to
support this section with a piece of lath. The slope corresponds
with the slope on the back section and is formed by turning up this
rear piece of cardboard. The shelter can extend out 6 inches and
the corners should be cut away as shown. Two struts of wood
sloped off, as in the sketch, will keep the shelter section firm

216

HOW TO MAKE A MODEL MOTOR GARAGE

Shown by dotted lines are the suggested strips of wood which will enable the doors to slide along. These strips should be made up of stripwood, $\frac{1}{2}$ inch wide and gummed to the underside of the shelter. Make the doors with flat sections of strong cardboard made just large enough to run along the grooves easily. Line these sections with wood-grained paper, allowing tiny windows 1 inch by 1 inch.

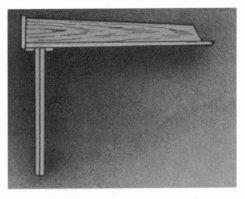

The elevation of the shelter, showing the doors and supports for the roof.

Do not make the doors too long, have several small sections.

The roof itself is made up from a large box lid and goes flat on to the supports at the back and the front. It overhangs at the rear by 1 inch and at the front by $1\frac{1}{2}$ inches. The panels are cut out to give extra light and are lined. These should be long and narrow, but not too big, otherwise your roof will crumple. This, and the shelter should be painted dull grey.

To give depth to the model the additional cardboard facia board should be fitted to a piece of lath and placed along the top of the main roof. Here is the place for the clock and the sundry advertisements, etc. A piece of thin dowel stuck in a cotton reel and painted in flat white paint will be ideal for a flagstaff, and will provide a finishing touch.

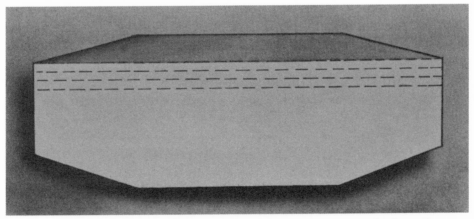

The front roof support and shelter. The shaded part turns up to take the roof.

HOW TO MAKE A MODEL MOTOR GARAGE

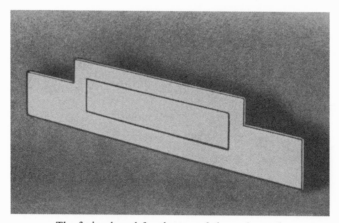

The facing board for the top of the main roof.

It may be found that the boxes on the ends may look rather shallow and unfinished. If this is so, it can be remedied by adding a further series of cardboard facia boards, which can be glued all round the front, back and along the outside edge. Take these up to about $2\frac{1}{2}$ inches and shape them as shown in the illustration. Paint these white and line the edges with black enamel, making the black band $\frac{1}{4}$ of an inch wide. If you can find small advertisements to fasten on these facia boards, they should be adopted.

The familiar island outside the garage can be made up with the lid of any box, such as a boot box. To save it sagging in the centre, fix in a couple of extra " L "-shaped pieces of cardboard underneath. Paint this in a grey shade and here you will have an ideal setting for the petrol pumps, which are obtainable in small boxes at toy shops. Lights under the shelter can be made from large, round, white beads suspended on straightened-out paper fasteners. A neat wall to make a surround should be made up with short lengths of plaster laths, painted grey. There are many uses for these laths, they can be had at any woodyard at a price of about twenty-four for one shilling.

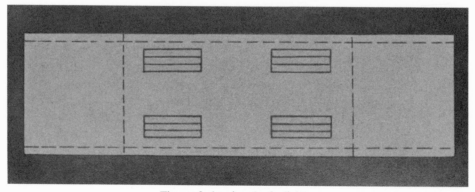

The roof, showing the fanlights.

218

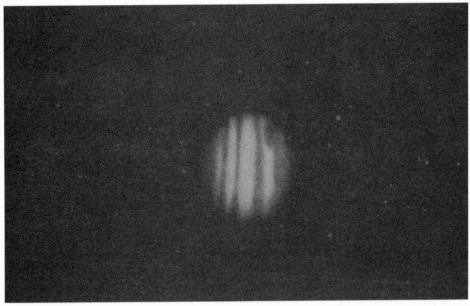

By courtesy of]　　　　　　　　　　　　　　[*The Royal Astronomical Society.*

JUPITER.

ADVENTURE AFTER DARK

WHEN the sun has set, and night has fallen, we seem to be looking on a new world. For darkness plays queer tricks with the imagination ; distances seem greater, familiar objects are often unrecognisable, trees and other quite normal things loom up gigantic and almost grotesque, birds and animals retire and their places are taken by others with nocturnal habits.

Particularly is this so in the country, where there are few lights to dispel the blackness . . . and it is at night time that one can capture a new thrill from a stalking or tracking expedition over ground that has become too familiar perhaps to hold much of interest by day.

There's plenty of adventure to be had on a hike on some clear, starry night—a new world, as it were, to explore—new subjects to interest the hiker—new discoveries to be made about things we have already explored in the day-time.

Among new activities which are opened up is the very fascinating study of the stars. Apart from their interest in themselves, a knowledge of the stars may be very useful to the night explorer. The old pioneers were able to steer a straight course over unknown and

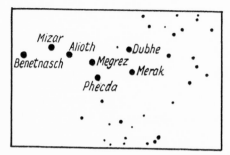

The Plough or Great Bear.
The stars Mizar and Dubhe are pointers
to the Pole Star.

trackless country by means of their knowledge of the stars and their positions in relation to the compass points. They knew, too, how to tell the time by the stars—and that is something everyone will find interesting, and maybe useful, to know.

Most stars visible in the sky form themselves into definite groups, known as constellations, and they remain always fixed in their positions with regard to each other. Since the Earth revolves once every twenty-four hours, these stars, like the sun, appear to move gradually round the Earth. Stars which are low down on the eastern horizon in the early evening gradually climb higher into the sky, while others sink towards—and eventually below—the western horizon.

The exceptions to these are the planets (wandering stars), which do not remain in fixed positions, but appear in varying places at different seasons of the year.

There are about 3,000 stars visible in our latitude, though they are not all visible at the same time.

There is one star which appears to us never to move at all—the Pole Star, which lies due North. In the northern hemisphere this is an invaluable guide to direction, and it can be located by means of the Plough (or Great Bear) Constellation.

The Plough consists of seven bright stars, the two which form the side of the " plough " opposite to the long " handle " are called Pointers, because they point in a straight line to the Pole Star. The Little Bear is another constellation close by, and the Pole Star is the last one in the "tail" of the "bear."

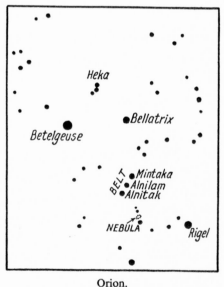

Orion.
The most brilliant of the equatorial constellations, and, after the Great Bear, probably the most familiar.

ADVENTURE AFTER DARK

In the southern hemisphere the Southern Cross constellation (not visible in our latitudes) indicates in a similar way the direction of the South Pole.

Another constellation useful for finding direction—and this one can be seen in both the northern *and* southern hemispheres—is Orion. This is supposed to represent a man wearing a sword and belt—and the three stars in the line (the belt) are easily recognisable. Three other stars (indicating the sword) can also be picked out . . . and the Pole Star is found in this case by joining up, with an imaginary line, the " sword " with the middle of the " head " of the man. This line, continued on above the head, leads directly to the North Star.

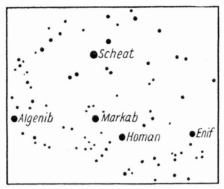
Pegasus—The Flying Horse.

Once having located the North in either of these ways, it is simple to point out the other compass directions, and to form some idea, at any rate, of the bearing of your objective.

The constellations which encircle the Pole Star are always visible in our latitude. Apart from these, in Spring you can see : Boōtes, the Herdsman ; Virgo, the Virgin ; and Scorpio, the Scorpion, with Antares (a red star).

In Summer there are visible : Aquila, the Eagle ; and Pegasus, the Flying Horse ; in Autumn, Taurus, the Bull ; Orion ; and Canis Major (marked by Sirius, the Dog Star).

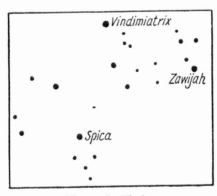
Virgo—the Virgin.
This contains the white first magnitude star Spica, or the Ear of Corn.

In Winter : Canis Minor, the Little Dog ; Gemini, the Twins ; and Leo, the Lion are to be seen.

These are but a few of the visible stars, but they are the most important because they are more or less the brightest and most conspicuous. With the aid of a star map, you will be able to pick them out without difficulty, and will then be able to continue this wonderful study for yourselves.

221

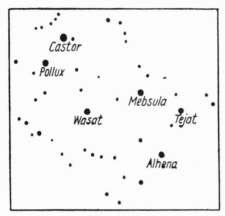

Gemini—The Twins.

Castor and Pollux are the brightest stars n this constellation.

There are several ways of telling the time by the stars, but perhaps the simplest is to imagine a line drawn across the sky as in the diagram. The three stars joined by this line always maintain the same position relative to each other, though they appear to move round the sky as already explained. You can imagine the line to be the hand of a clock, indicating " star time " on a 24-hour dial. The hand, however, " moves " in an anti-clockwise direction, and its imaginary position at various times is shown by the diagram.

At the Spring Equinox—March 21st—this star time is identical with sun time, but for the rest of the year it varies, and must be adjusted as follows :

From the " star time " estimated from the position of the hand in the sky :

Subtract 4 minutes for each day after March 21st.

Subtract half-an-hour for each week after March 21st.

Subtract two hours for each month after March 21st.

The result will give approximately sun time as from mid-day . . . but during the summer months this will need adjusting an hour to bring it into line with British Summer Time.

A knowledge of the stars is thus by way of being a great help to the pioneer and explorer, as well as proving useful and interesting.

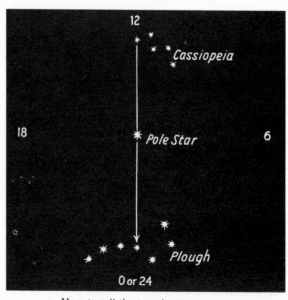

How to tell the time by the stars.

[*Mount Wilson Observatory.*

STAR CLOUDS IN SAGITTARIUS.

HOW TO RUN A TREASURE HUNT

THE general idea of a treasure hunt is the tracking down of some " treasure " (such as a box of chocolates, a bag of fruit or a small present), by means of clues like those discovered by detectives.

The organiser must first decide on the place where he is hiding the " treasure." This can easily be in a house, a shed in a garden, or even a shop where the organiser meets the winner and buys him or her the " treasure." Having hidden the " treasure " the organiser proceeds to provide a guide to the clues in the following manner :

Under the big oak tree beyond a trim garden, a flower hides the first important clue. (This might mean that the clue is buried under a specially-planted flower under a tree that should be known to all hunters.)

Pass along a straight road near where stands a ragged man. He has the second clue to the treasure. (This could mean that the hunters must search the pockets of a scarecrow in a field.)

Other clues might be concealed in the branches of a low tree ; left in a vase of the organiser's house ; attached to a lamp-post, or hidden in an empty water-butt.

There should be about ten or a dozen clues, and as each hunter finds a clue, he must replace it exactly as he found it, ready for the next arrival. Many a hunt has been ruined because some eager hunter has failed to do this.

The organiser of a treasure hunt must not make the instructions too easy or too difficult ; and he can vary the excitement by putting half a clue in a hiding-place and leaving the hunters to find the other portion elsewhere. An instance of this kind of clue would be a bicycle lamp with the organiser's name on it, an object that is meant to lead the hunters to his home and to the cycle shed.

One important point—you must impress upon everyone that no ground has to be dug up, otherwise your competitors may find themselves interfering with other people's property in their enthusiasm as amateur detectives.

All clues must be named before the " treasure " is handed over.

[*Frontispiece.*

CHEMICAL EXPERIMENTS.

A YOUNG MOUNTAINEER.

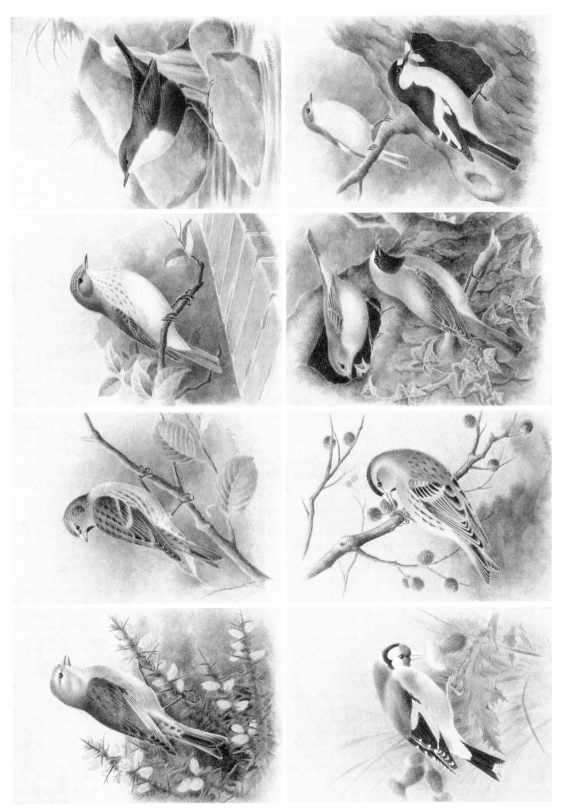

SOME BRITISH BIRDS.

Top—left to right: LINNET, LESSER REDPOLL, SPOTTED FLYCATCHER, DIPPER.

Bottom—left to right: GOLDFINCH, SISKIN, REDSTART, PIED FLYCATCHER.

THE MODEL RAILWAY.

WILD FLOWERS. 1. Dog Rose.   2. Orchis.   3. Teasel.   4. Marsh Marigold.   5. Foxglove.
6. Harebell.   7. Cuckoo Pint.   8. Monk's Hood.   9. Primrose.   10. Poppy.   11. Sweet Violet.

A RURAL RIDE.

THE SWIMMING POOL.

MAKING A TOY CRANE.